The Golden Horseshoe

The Golden Horseshoe

The Life and Times of the Metropolitan Opera House

by the editors of *Opera News*

Frank Merkling

John W. Freeman

Gerald Fitzgerald

with Arthur Solin

Prologue by Eleanor R. Belmont

Epilogue by Anthony A. Bliss

A Studio Book   The Viking Press   New York

Art direction and design by Arthur Solin

First published in 1965 by The Viking Press, Inc.
625 Madison Avenue, New York, N. Y. 10022

Published simultaneously in Canada by
The Macmillan Company of Canada Limited

Printed in U.S.A. by the Halliday Lithograph Corp.
Library of Congress catalog card number: 65-24512

Contents

Each chapter is keyed to a particular season that brought some significant alteration to the Opera House structure; interrupting this chronological sequence are three Entr'actes and an Encore, which are organized by subject matter.

Acknowledgments

This book is a collective effort. It could not have been completed without the generous assistance of many hands.

First, the photographs. Special acknowledgment is due to Alexandre Georges for his portfolio of pictures of the Opera House itself. For most of the color pictures of current productions the authors are indebted to Frank Dunand, photographer for the Metropolitan Opera Guild's Education Department, and to its director, Robert A. Tuggle. Complete picture credits appear on page 319.

Second, the text. Mary Ellis Peltz, archivist of the Metropolitan Opera, and Francis Robinson, assistant manager in charge of its press department, have given unstintingly of their time and advice at various stages of the manuscript. Douglass M. Allen has contributed experienced judgment, taste, and wit to the final organization and tightening of the text.

Finally, the project as a whole. We are grateful for the guidance and support of the Publications Committee of the Metropolitan Opera Board of Directors: Lowell Wadmond, Chairman; Lauder Greenway, *ex officio*; Malcolm Muir; Mrs. August Belmont; and Reginald Allen.

To mention Mrs. Belmont's name next to last may seem ungallant, but in the tradition of the theater this spot on the program was reserved for the star—one whom we would single out for special thanks. Without her encouragement, criticism, and unfaltering faith in our efforts there might never have been a book at all.

Frank Merkling
John W. Freeman
Gerald Fitzgerald
Arthur Solin

Prologue

by Eleanor R. Belmont

Grand opera is not native to the United States. It was imported—composers, interpreters, bag and baggage—fully armed from the soil of Europe. Wealthy, traveled Americans, and foreign-born citizens who made this country their own, collected the best specimens of art they could find to adorn their homes and communities. They also endeavored to establish and support grand opera here. These music-minded pioneers, like so many other builders of America, were men whose roots had been transplanted from the Old World. The love of opera was latent in their hearts, even when they lived in a new land rough-hewing a culture of its own.

An opera house with a resident company in it was at once a symbol and a heritage to these late-nineteenth-century New Yorkers. They had inherited or acquired great wealth and were prepared to assume the responsibility of an art patronage which, in the lands of their forefathers, had been the obligation and prerogative of royal individuals or the state. Americans of wealth at this same time and thereafter were to build museums and libraries and were to fill them with treasures of painting, sculpture, and printing; and even were to build—stone by stone—chapels, palaces, and cloisters, all brought from overseas.

With the city's growth in population, grand opera moved from house to house in New York. In 1883, to accommodate increasing public interest, the Metropolitan Opera House opened its doors. This plain-faced structure was financed by a group of rich New Yorkers who purchased stock in the cultural enterprise, and each received in return a Parterre Box for the use of themselves, their families, descendants, and friends.

Thus it was grand opera, not the House, that was the true objective. It was grand opera that for fifty-seven years these Metropolitan Opera House stockholders sponsored (and supported, when necessary), while the Directors of the Metropolitan Opera Association who succeeded them, aided by occasional local and later national drives for funds, carried on a support made essential by difficult times and ever-rising deficits. However, a new era began for the Metropolitan Opera House twenty-five years ago, when it was purchased from private ownership and became a national trust.

Assembled from the world's best talent, this great Company has been largely responsible for the appreciation of opera that is spreading like a flame across the country. The Metropolitan is unique in that, unlike every other national opera house in the world, it has no government subsidy. It has survived because thousands of listeners annually pay their loyal tribute to support it—with the notable assistance since 1935 of the Metropolitan Opera

Guild, and in late years from the National Council. When there is hunger for great music, music will survive. Pomp and circumstance may have faded somewhat from the audience, yet unquestionably on stage the beauty and the glamour remain.

The listening audience must be forever grateful for broadcast performances from the Metropolitan, initiated by David Sarnoff and generously sponsored for the past twenty-five years by Texaco Inc., which have made operatic music of imperishable beauty available to it. Without the modern miracle of radio, millions of Americans would never have experienced the pleasure and the spiritual exaltation of great opera. Records and broadcasting have rapidly made ours a nation of music-lovers. Who knows what future flowering may spring from these seeds? Through the efforts of the Guild, opera has been brought into the high schools and colleges, and youth has learned that in addition to cultural enrichment and intellectual exercise, grand opera is first-class entertainment.

Looking back over three-quarters of a century, one is poignantly aware of the various and drastic changes that have taken place in the world, changes more profound in their meaning, perhaps, than those of any comparable period of history. Science has advanced across the earth in seven-league boots, producing effects that would have been incredible seventy-five years ago, while empires, beliefs, conventions—centuries old—have gone from the scene. Strangely enough, opera has not only survived the world turmoil, it has prevailed, although at no period has it been self-supporting.

Grand opera at the Metropolitan has had its ups and downs, accompanied by human errors of omission and commission. Yet each decade has revealed some peak of achievement to which the Company may point with some considerable pride. A lack of adequate financing has been a major handicap, as crisis followed crisis and two world wars confronted all the arts with tragic problems. Inevitably, the wars took a heavy toll of potential artists. No one can ever measure the loss sustained as a result of the wholesale slaughter of youth during those grim years.

Frequently we hear sighs of regret for the "golden age" of opera. What makes a golden age? During recent years, glittering performances—the miraculous coordination of a splendid orchestra and chorus, and superb soaring solo voices—have been given of fine new productions at the Metropolitan. Drama has crossed Broadway and formed a closer relationship with opera than we have ever seen.

This Prologue is written in a nostalgic mood. After eighty-three extraordinary years in the House on Thirty-ninth Street, the Metropolitan Opera Company will move to a splendid edifice at Sixty-fourth Street in the heart of Lincoln Center, a change that marks the end of an era. Nostalgia for the past is eclipsed by hope for the future. As long as histories of the Metropolitan are written, anno Domini 1966 will be remembered. The present book assembles as an *aide-mémoire* a cluster of high spots in the life of this noble institution.

When the immensely difficult transfer to Lincoln Center is made, the old House, a disintegrating shell, will be left behind, and memories of the "beloved hall with music ringing" will surge through the minds of loyal friends, who for so long have found happiness there. But these memories, as well as the high hopes and firm faith of an opera-minded multitude, will follow the Company to its new home. As the eventful exodus approaches, let us salute a record of splendid achievement. Let us salute the dedicated Board members, the skillful opera management, the hardworking, ofttimes fabulous artists, American and foreign, onstage and in the pit, who have brought our national Company international fame.

The golden age of opera confronts a new era. Everyone who has experienced the thrill of superb opera performances knows in his heart the answer to a poet's question, "Who dreamed that beauty passes like a dream?" True beauty does *not* pass; mysteriously it is recorded, and while memory lasts it is stamped indelibly in the mind and in the heart. The vibrant soul of the Company will always be the essential factor—wherever the Metropolitan Opera Company may make its home.

Introduction

The Metropolitan Opera House has outlived its competition. More and more at odds with her frankly commercial surroundings, the Grand Old Lady of Thirty-ninth Street has survived, somehow, in a rapidly changing New York in which all her rivals have been replaced by hotels, office buildings, and department stores.

The patrician Academy of Music, at Fourteenth Street and Irving Place, has long since given way to a skyscraper, the Consolidated Edison Building, whose illuminated cupola recalls the day when the Union Square area was New York's entertainment center. (The Academy's name is preserved in a Fourteenth Street movie house opposite the historic site.) The corner of Herald Square on which Oscar Hammerstein's old Manhattan Opera House stood is now occupied by Macy's; the great showman might have been pleased to see his creation superseded by "the world's largest store." The newer Manhattan Opera House, farther west on Thirty-fourth Street, which goaded the Metropolitan into some of its greatest activity, has been rebuilt as Manhattan Center, a complex of ballrooms and banquet halls. And the Summit, a serpentine structure faced with green brick—first of a rash of new hotels to be erected in New York in the 1960's—has lately replaced the Lexington Theater, recently a movie house, at Fifty-first Street and Lexington Avenue, where Hammerstein tried for a fresh start in 1913.

The New Theater, erected at Sixty-second Street and Central Park West in the 1900's, which served as an adjunct to the Metropolitan, failed at this function but enjoyed a long life as the Century Theater, and bequeathed this name to a twin-towered apartment house on its original site, as well as to another theater three blocks south. Even Otto Kahn's unbuilt "new Metropolitan," on West Fifty-seventh Street, left imposing traces: Joseph Urban, who had been working on the plans, designed the Hearst Magazine Building that materialized at the corner of Eighth Avenue, and the site intended for the opera house was eventually utilized for the enormous apartment complex known as Parc Vendôme.

Meanwhile, the old Metropolitan has stood fast, adapting its outmoded frame as best it could to the demands of each succeeding era. The shift that has taken place within its eighty-three-year life span, causing the operatic center of gravity to move two and a half miles up Broadway, from Union Square to Herald Square to Times Square and past Columbus Circle to Lincoln Square, has been paralleled by a revolution—that is, one full turn—in taste. It is to the Metropolitan's lasting credit that its history has mirrored, if not led, this change.

The Metropolitan has had seven active managers since it

opened in 1883: Henry E. Abbey, Leopold Damrosch, Maurice Grau, Heinrich Conried, Giulio Gatti-Casazza, Edward Johnson, and Rudolf Bing. (Four others held the title: Edmund Stanton carried out Damrosch's program after his death; John Schoeffel and Andreas Dippel were silent partners; and Herbert Witherspoon died before he could prove the effectiveness of his plans.) Of the seven, one was American, one German, one Italian, and one Canadian; three came from Austria or Austrian-dominated areas of Europe. In general these managers epitomized a trend away from the provincial and in the direction of the cosmopolitan; as a consequence, the term of each manager has tended to be longer and more complex than that of his predecessor. (Not one of the holders of the office has outlived his tenure by more than nine years.)

The Metropolitan's development has gone through six stages, not quite corresponding to the terms of the seven managers. During its first decade (1883–1893), the languages in which the operas were performed—first Italian, then German, then French—betokened a national bias based on the origins or connections of the man in charge. Since the aim of the boxholders was at least partly social, one alien tongue onstage sufficed as well as another, so long as the total result proved diverting. Next came a decade of rule (and unruliness) by the singers, the so-called Golden Age (1893–1903), during which all three languages were utilized. (As late as 1896–1897, however, it was still possible to hear *Die Meistersinger* performed in Italian translation.) In the following period of a dozen years (1903–1915), beginning in Conried's term, respect for the score—orchestral as well as vocal—was the ruling passion of a handful of outstanding conductors. Operas were now given in the original language, except for Czech and Russian. And the repertory had been liberalized along with the audience.

A fourth phase, following the onset of World War I, paradoxically began with two decades of peace in the Opera House (1915–1935) and, save for the final years, of prosperity; the formula, which Gatti-Casazza might have imported from ancient Rome, balanced bread (evenly doled-out staple repertory fare) with circuses (handsomely mounted novelties). If an emphasis on *mise en scène* supplanted music drama in the performances of these years, which saw little Mozart, Beethoven, or Gluck, still the Metropolitan was crowded with season-ticket subscribers.

After 1931, however, it became essential to find new sources of income. Two of these, the radio audience and the Opera Guild, enabled the Company to ride out the Depression years and the Second World War years that followed, and even to develop a more unified ensemble. Johnson's fifteen-year regime (1935–1950) was succeeded by that of Rudolf Bing, whose devotion to good theater has offset postwar increases in the cost of labor by raising the average attendance to 97.2 per cent of capacity, doubling the number of subscribers, and increasing the length of the season to a record twenty-nine weeks. Meanwhile, new practitioners of *bel canto*—the style in vogue when the Opera House opened—have arisen, notably Maria Callas and Joan Sutherland.

For the first twenty-five years of its existence, control of the Metropolitan was vested absolutely in the boxholders, who owned the Opera House and leased it to an impresario. In 1908 a new system of divided control was instituted, with the older faction continuing for thirty-two years, until 1940, to rule on policy while granting autonomy on production to a new company headed by Otto Kahn. For the past twenty-six years this second company, having bought out the first, has comprised both Church and State: the power has passed from an oligarchy to an enlightened Croesus to the ticket-buyer.

A certain symmetry is apparent in these phases of the Metropolitan's history. The year in which the first official mention was made of the need for a new opera house, 1924, was exactly the halfway point in the existence of the old Metropolitan. Affection for the stately maroon-and-gold theater, whose Edwardian elegance has recently returned to fashion, cannot obscure the hard fact that at least half its life has been lived under the shadow of technical and economic obsolescence. The ground on which it stands has become increasingly valuable commercially; rent from this property, once the building is razed, will help the Metropolitan Opera Company to serve a wider audience, and serve it better, at Lincoln Center, where air-conditioning and television facilities are built into the plans for the new opera house.

Whatever lofty structure replaces the Metropolitan when it is torn down will be dwarfed by an even loftier edifice of memory. For these old walls have sheltered the most glittering audiences, most of the finest singers and conductors, and many of the most impressive spectacles of opera seen anywhere in the past hundred years. The resident Company alone has staged some ten thousand performances there, comprising more than two hundred operas. If success is the ratio of ends—what has been accomplished—to means provided, the Metropolitan Opera House must be ranked as something of a miracle.

The New Yellow Brewery

In New York in the spring of 1880—when Madison Square was the heart of the city, and goats grazed north of Fifty-ninth Street —selling the Brooklyn Bridge, unfinished though it was, was as likely a transaction as buying a box at the opera, and perhaps easier.

There was no novelty about grand opera to account for the sudden bullish market in gilt-edged chairs. Opera had been presented sporadically in New York ever since 1825, and on a regular seasonal basis since the completion in 1854 of the Academy of Music on Irving Place. What was new was the burgeoning number of New Yorkers who could afford boxes. The Academy, as it happened, was short on boxes, and the most desirable had been pre-empted by families long accustomed to wealth and social prestige. The Old Guard, known to society writers as the "Faubourg St. Germain set," had no wish to see the newly affluent and culture-conscious excluded. It simply did not propose to see itself excluded in order to accommodate them.

On April 3, 1880, a committee of directors of the Academy, composed of the Messrs. August Belmont (chairman), Dinsmore, Lorillard, and Hoffman, received Mr. George Henry Warren, envoy of the boxholders *manqués*. Warren asked for more new boxes than the auditorium would hold: the Vanderbilts (W. H., W. K., and Cornelius) alone needed five, and George Henry Warren and Robert and Ogden Goelet each wanted two. Also seeking boxes, but willing to settle for one per clan, were Bakers, Fields, Frenches, Goulds, Iselins, Morgans, Rhinelanders, Whitneys, and so on and on; the aggregate fortunes of the families concerned came to some $540,000,000. The Academy directors agreed to construct twenty-six new boxes—the best they could do in the available space—but this was not nearly enough, and a few weeks later the well-heeled have-nots announced the formation of the Metropolitan Opera-house Company, Ltd., to build a new theater for grand opera.

The founders—fifty-two at the start, and soon to number seventy—subscribed $10,000 apiece, or 100 shares of stock at $100 per share, as warranty for their boxes, and set about finding a proper site for the new opera house. The quest, considering the city's vast reaches of undeveloped real estate and the combined resources of the shareholders, proved surprisingly difficult. For one thing, it was impossible to summon a quorum at any meeting during the summer, a problem that might have been overcome by holding the meetings in Newport, Rhode Island, instead of New

York City. W. H. Vanderbilt, trying to be helpful, did offer, at bargain prices, one and later another appealing parcel of New York Central Railroad property. But both of these proved to be covered by restrictive covenants of which Vanderbilt had been unaware, prohibiting the building of a "place of entertainment" on the site. The more attractive of the two was the block bounded by Madison and Vanderbilt Avenues and Forty-third and Forty-fourth Streets, where the Hotel Biltmore now stands. Vanderbilt asked $300,000 for this and estimated that the restriction could be bought off for another $65,000. The shareholders demurred at the added cost of either this or the other Vanderbilt offering and wound up paying $605,000 for the block between Broadway and Seventh Avenue and Thirty-ninth and Fortieth Streets. That was only their first lesson in the economics of opera. Before they heard a note of music, the Bowery Savings Bank had their mortgage note, and the price of a box had risen to $15,000.

While the site was being selected, the founders invited four architectural firms to submit competitive designs and sealed bids, those rejected to receive $1,000 each. All four firms gave fanciful names to their designs, but the winning entry was *Lyre,* which invoked the Muse while suggesting the traditional horseshoe shape of the auditorium. Josiah Cleaveland Cady, nominal creator of *Lyre,* was noted for his churches and college buildings, as well as the American Museum of Natural History. Never mind that he had never been in an opera house in his life: he designed one that boasted 122 boxes! His assistant and later partner, Louis de Coppet Bergh, may have had more to do with the plans than Cady; in any case, Cady is known to have summoned Bergh back from his wedding trip with a series of urgent telegrams soon after the contract was awarded. Cady had never been abroad. Bergh had, to study in Stuttgart, but the stern background he shared with his employer had confined his musical knowledge to the church organ.

Once engaged, however, Cady and Bergh overcame whatever scruples they had about opera and bent to their task with a will, hiring extra draftsmen and office space. They consulted pictures and plans of major European theaters and chose the Royal Opera House in Covent Garden, London, as the model for their auditorium, which also incorporated features of La Scala and other famous houses. The Bayreuth Festspielhaus, opened seven years before, they considered too small to use as a model. A pity, for it boasted nearly perfect sight lines; though Cady and Bergh made some seven hundred drawings in an effort to insure good sight lines in their auditorium, they came up with almost precisely that number of seats whose view of the stage is obstructed. Cantile-

---

William Henry Vanderbilt (1821–1885), president of the New York Central Railroad, in a portrait by Eastman Johnson. He was son of the "Commodore" and father of William K., also a Metropolitan stockholder.

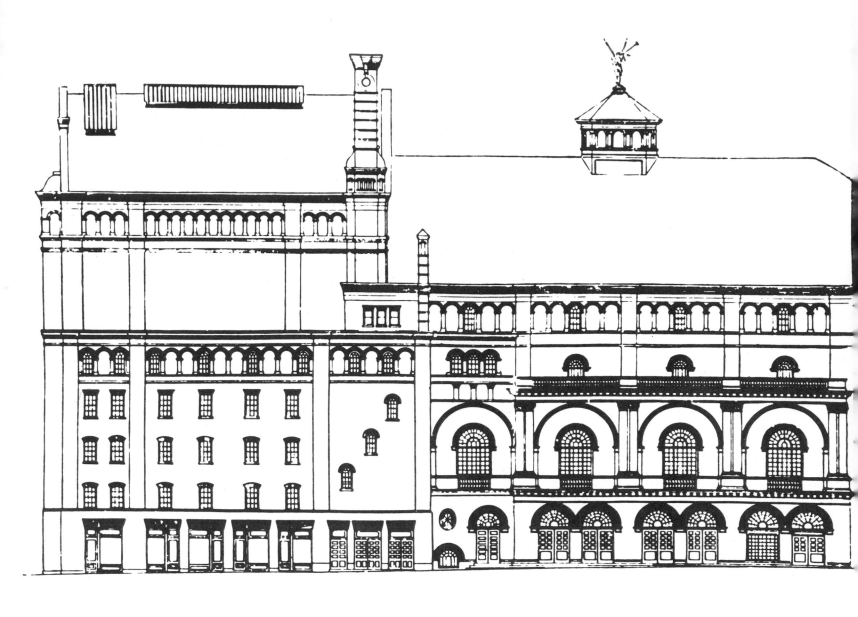

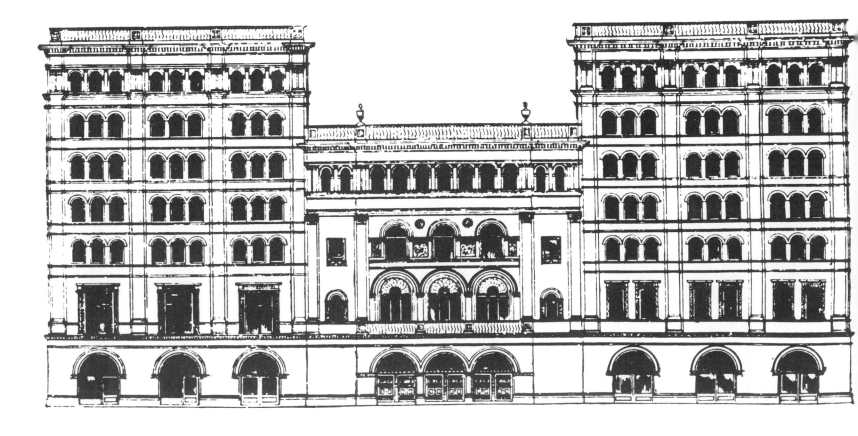

The men who designed the Metropolitan:
Josiah Cleaveland Cady (*below left*) and his
assistant, Louis de Coppet Bergh, may have
known nothing about opera, but the firm had
made a name for itself designing façades in
Early Renaissance style, including fifteen
buildings at Yale and the American Museum of
Natural History (1877, *left*). The elevations
for the Opera House (*opposite page*) show a
shell fit for the latter-day Medici—top, the
Thirty-ninth Street façade, dominated by a
decorative air vent and the windows of what
was to be the Metropolitan Opera Club; below,
the main front on Broadway, flanked by office
towers.

Contemporary monuments: The streets of New York in 1884, when the earliest known photograph of the Metropolitan (*opposite page*) was taken, were lined with cables, paved with cobblestones, and grooved with trolley tracks. To the south, in New York Harbor, the Statue of Liberty was being assembled on Bedloe's Island (*above*); the world's longest suspension span, Brooklyn Bridge (*left*), had opened just five months before the Opera House.

vered balconies of structural steel were about to be invented—not, unfortunately, by Cady and Bergh. The sight lines of the Metropolitan became known as among the worst in major opera houses, although its acoustics, enhanced by an oval sounding shell of masonry beneath the orchestra pit, proved to be among the best.

To provide the number of boxes that was his employers' first concern, Cady designed what was then the largest auditorium in the world. Behind a modified Italian Renaissance façade, with ordered rows of Romanesque windows, was a five-story house, with three of the tiers in the horseshoe lined with boxes, and twelve *baignoire* boxes (shaped like old-fashioned tin bathtubs) on the orchestra floor for good measure. Altogether the boxes accounted for 732 seats, or a whopping 24 per cent of the house's 3,045.

In an effort to make the gaslit building fireproof, Cady relied heavily on brick, tile, and iron in its construction. Even the roof and proscenium arch were of iron, as was the intricate web of 4,000 struts on which the stage rested. The stage itself was suitably large—106 feet wide, 86 feet deep, and 125 feet high; only the Paris Opéra and the Imperial Opera in St. Petersburg had larger stages. In his innocence of what goes on in a theater, however, the architect failed to provide adequate rehearsal rooms or storage space for scenery.

The interior decoration was assigned to E. P. Treadwell of Boston, with an admonition from the architect to "avoid all tawdriness or garish display." Treadwell carpeted the auditorium in warm red, draped the boxes with curtains of old gold and the stage with a curtain of deep blue, gilded the box fronts to create the "Golden Horseshoe" and tinted the walls a slightly reddish orange, the woodwork and ceiling ivory. Francis Lathrop's painting of Apollo and the Muses, surrounded by Francis Maynard's figures of the Ballet and Chorus, graced the proscenium, and figures of cherubs gamboled on the pilasters.

On May 24, 1883, the proud new opera house was opened to the sixty-five Metropolitan shareholders—five having defected from their peak number of seventy—for inspection and the drawing of boxes by lot. They were delighted with what they saw: a handsome house with boxes galore. But "Colonel" James Mapleson, impresario of the old Academy of Music, snorted at that "new yellow brewery on Broadway."

He would shortly discover just how yeasty it was.

London's Royal Opera House, Covent Garden, dating in its present form (*opposite page*) from 1858, supplied a model for the Metropolitan's auditorium, augmented by details from Milan's Scala (*right*).

20

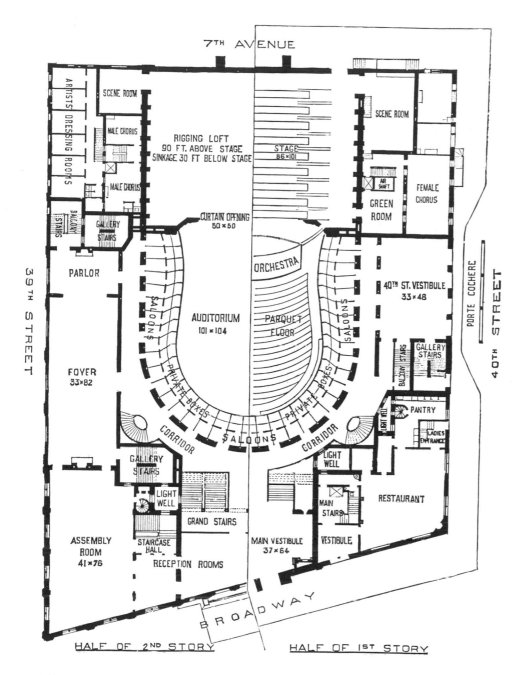

Labels in floor plan:

7TH AVENUE

ARTISTS' DRESSING ROOMS

SCENE ROOM

MALE CHORUS

RIGGING LOFT
90 FT. ABOVE STAGE
SINKAGE 30 FT BELOW STAGE

STAGE
86×101

SCENE ROOM

MALE CHORUS

AIR SHAFT

FEMALE CHORUS

GREEN ROOM

BALCONY STAIRS

GALLERY STAIRS

CURTAIN OPENING
50×50

PARLOR

ORCHESTRA

40TH ST. VESTIBULE
33×48

39TH STREET

SALOONS

AUDITORIUM
101×104

PARQUET FLOOR

PRIVATE BOXES

SALOONS

40TH STREET

PORTE COCHERE

GALLERY STAIRS

BALCONY STAIRS

FOYER
33×82

PRIVATE BOXES

PANTRY

LIGHT WELL

LADIES ENTRANCE

CORRIDOR

SALOONS

CORRIDOR

LIGHT WELL

GALLERY STAIRS

LIGHT WELL

RESTAURANT

GRAND STAIRS

MAIN STAIRS

ASSEMBLY ROOM
41×76

STAIRCASE HALL

RECEPTION ROOMS

MAIN VESTIBULE
37×64

VESTIBULE

BROADWAY

HALF OF 2ND STORY   HALF OF 1ST STORY

Not models for the Metropolitan: Though the Paris Opéra (*opposite page*) had opened in 1875, its superb public spaces found no counterpart in the Metropolitan's cramped corridors and meager halls; nor did the Metropolitan reflect the democratic, unsurpassed sightlines of the Bayreuth Festspielhaus (*below*), opened in 1876, or its huge stage house. The floor plan at left shows the two reasons: the large number of boxes presupposed a large auditorium, and the site filling a city block prevented the Metropolitan from ever being enlarged.

A House of Princes
1883–1884

As the sun disappeared behind the seven-story towers and darkness crept up the Broadway façade, gas lights fluttered on to illuminate the foyer and marquee. Soon windows brightened by twos and threes, marking the progress of lamplighters from chamber to chamber of the sprawling new structure, until all four bordering streets glowed. Then the brilliance of the auditorium chandelier—an immense ring of gas flame—penetrated the skylight and cast a kind of halo in the dusk. For the first time the Metropolitan Opera House had come magically to life.

It was opening night, October 22, 1883, a night the curious neighborhood had anticipated as keenly as the Metropolitan's sponsors and opera devotees in general. Clerks and stenographers lingered in the building just across Fortieth Street for "opening night" office parties; lumberyard workers in the next block headed for a convenient bar to await the excitement; and the girls in the squalid two-story houses on Thirty-ninth Street, known as "Soubrettes' Row," leaned out of their windows hoping for once to see rather than be seen.

Two blocks up Broadway, at Forty-second Street, the elegant saloons of the Hotels St. Cloud and Metropole swarmed with gay groups, opera-bound, in evening dress, and one block down Broadway the Hotel Normandie rang with vocalizing as visiting singers, headed for the bright side of the footlights, did their final warming-up in their rooms.

Outside the Opera House, near the boxholders' porte-cochère on Thirty-ninth Street, crowds gathered to watch the arrival of the *haut monde*—the men dashing in top hats, opera capes with red velvet linings, and white ties and tailcoats, their starched shirts studded with pearls; the ladies resplendent in tiaras of emeralds and diamonds, parures to match, and ermine, sable, or chinchilla wraps. They came in shiny broughams, victorias, and cabriolets with crests glistening on the doors, driven by liveried coachmen, attended by footmen, and drawn by high-stepping horses that clopped daintily over the cobbles.

The opera was Gounod's *Faust,* in Italian, with the familiar Swedish soprano Christine Nilsson as "Margherita." Impresario Henry E. Abbey had fixed 6:45 as curtain time. Ticketholders pressed into the new house early to examine its décor and gasped at its expanse; but the arrival of some of the owners, who as shareholders had already inspected the premises, was less prompt.

The Metropolitan's first manager, Henry E. Abbey (wearing boater), on vacation at Henley-on-Thames, England, with his wife, Edith, and their friends, Captain and Mrs. Bainbridge (photo dated July 2, 1885).

When Abbey noticed that the Golden Horseshoe was not yet filled, he prudently delayed the curtain, and it was 7:15 before Maestro Auguste Vianesi of London's Covent Garden rapped his baton on the music stand and spread his arms for the opening downbeat. Five and a half hours later the final notes of *Faust* were followed by deafening applause and passionate cries of *brava* and *bravo.* While the cast bowed and curtsied in various combinations through a long series of curtain calls, ushers wheeled cartloads of flowers down the aisles and burdened the happily weary stars. Mme. Nilsson was singled out for a gold wreath, and as Signor Vianesi took his bow the orchestra rose in tribute.

Whether by accident or design, Abbey had hit upon an ingenious plan for opening night. The very long opera, relieved by four intermissions, gave his sponsors maximum time for social activity, and they moved from box to box and tier to tier, exuberantly toasting the opera and one another in magnums of Dom Pérignon.

This extracurricular gaiety was by no means confined to intermissions (nor was it to be for some years, until a reform was effected). Champagne corks popped and glasses clinked and social calls were exchanged throughout the performance—to the delight of neck-craning wealth-watchers and the dismay of opera-lovers in less exalted seats. Each box had its own spacious anteroom, which served as cloakroom and private lounge and from the start proved an ideal place for an eligible swain, holding an Orchestra ticket or less, to call upon the nubile daughter of the box-owner and, in the European tradition, offer himself as escort to a post-opera ball. If there happened to be a spare seat in the box, so much the better.

The constant comings and goings were not even confined to the new Opera House. To compete with the glamorous opening, the Academy of Music was presenting Mme. Nilsson's archrival, Etelka Gerster, in her most celebrated role, Amina in *La Sonnambula.* The roster of Metropolitan subscribers included a number who traditionally supported the Academy and had not yet determined their final allegiance; some of these commuted between the two houses throughout the evening. To add to the contretemps caused by competing operas, through some malevolent fate, or through human malice, what was to become the annual National Horse Show opened that same night; an appearance there was obligatory for some of the opera patrons. A few, like the ubiquitous Mrs. Paran Stevens, made the rounds of all three events.

Despite such hectic circumstances, the Metropolitan's first performance succeeded. "Nothing was shirked," wrote critic Henry

METROPOLITAN
OPERA HOUSE.

MR. HENRY E. ABBEY, - - - - - - - Director·
Acting Manager, - - - - - - MR. MAURICE GRAU.

MONDAY EVENING, OCTOBER 22, 1883,

INAUGURAL NIGHT
AND
First Night of the Subscription,
WHEN GOUNOD'S OPERA OF

"FAUST."

Will be presented with the following Cast:

FAUST,	Sig. ITALO CAMPANINI
MEPHISTOPHELES,	Sig. FRANCO NOVARA
VALENTINO,	Sig. GIUSEPPE DEL PUENTE
WAGNER,	Sig. CONTINI
SIEBEL,	Mme. SOFIA SCALCHI
MARTA,	Mlle. LOUISE LABLACHE

(Who has kindly consented to assume the part at short notice.   Her first appearance.)
AND
MARGHERITA, - - - - Mme. CHRISTINE NILSSON

Musical Director and Conductor, · Sig. VIANESI

WEBER PIANO USED.

Mason & Hamlin's Organ Used.

All the above Operas performed at this House can be had in every form, Vocal and Instrumental at G. SCHIRMER, No. 35 Union Square, Importer and Publisher of Music.

The Scenery by Messrs. Fox, Schaeffer, Maeder, and Thompson.
The Costumes are entirely new, and were manufactured at Venice by D. Ascoli
The Appointments by Mr. Bradwell.
Machinists, Messrs. Lundy & Gifford.

NIGHTLY PRICES OF ADMISSION:

Boxes, holding six (6) seats	$50
Orchestra Stalls	6
Balcony Stalls	3
Family Circle (reserved)	2
Admission to Family Circle	1

Seats and Boxes can be secured at the Box Office of the Metropolitan Opera House, which will remain open daily from 8 A. M. to 5 P. M.

Doors open at 7.15.   **Performances at 8 precisely**

Gunerius Gabrielson & Son, Florists to the Metropolitan Opera House.

Opera Glasses on Hire in the Lobby.

L. F. Mazette, Caterer.
Parties desiring Ices can be supplied by the Waiter, in Corridor.

Business Manager - - - - - - - - - - Mr. W. W. TILLOTSON.
Treasurer - - - - - - - - - - Mr. CHAS. H. MATHEWS.

The stars of opening night: The performance of *Faust* that inaugurated the Metropolitan featured the tenor Campanini (*top left*) in the title role, the soprano Nilsson as "Margherita," the bass Novara (an Englishman whose real name was Frank Nash) as "Mefistofele," and the contralto Scalchi in the trouser role of Siébel. The program (*opposite page*) included a reproduction of music-making cherubs in the Florentine style but no mention of what was taken for granted: the language sung was not French but Italian.

Krehbiel in the morning *Tribune,* "and the highest skill and most delicate ingenuity seemed combined in constructing scenes of fascinating beauty and almost perfect illusion." To be sure, Nilsson was "past the first flush of youth" and did not warm up until the Jewel Song; the Faust, Italo Campanini, sang poorly. But it was a triumph for Henry Abbey. Although a leading theatrical entrepreneur, Abbey was as new to grand opera as to the house itself. The Metropolitan directors had retained him to present sixty performances of what his contract called "first-class Italian opera" in return for a year's rent-free lease on the house and a guarantee of $1,000 per performance against losses.

By "Italian opera" both parties to the contract meant works lending themselves to *bel canto,* and sung in Italian, whatever their original language. This was a common convention of the time, because nearly every libretto was available in Italian translation; the language had become standard, since the number of outstanding singers with broad multilingual repertories was limited.

Abbey's musical background consisted of having played cornet in a high-school band in his native Akron, Ohio; but his musical taste was well developed, and his showmanship established beyond question. To costume all nineteen operas he was to produce, he commissioned the famous Parisian designer Worth, who had recently attained columns of newspaper space in the United States and set American womanhood atwitter by decreeing that "stuffed birds will be high in favor this spring, worn on the left shoulder with a cluster of flowers on evening dresses, or on dainty opera muffs."

Abbey knew how to gauge the attraction of stars, and he was not innocent of publicity values. His judgment of singers, apparent in his choice of Mme. Nilsson for opening night, was confirmed when Marcella Sembrich, a twenty-five-year-old Galician soprano who had already conquered Covent Garden, sang the title role in the Metropolitan's second production, *Lucia di Lammermoor.* The young artist—or her manager—had demanded that an advance of $30,000 be deposited in her London bank before she embarked from England; but she need not have feared being stranded in the United States. "No singer ever won the recognition of a New York audience more easily," wrote W. J. Henderson in the *Times,* after her debut.

Sembrich went on to sing nine other roles with equal success and became a mainstay of the initial season. But it was in the sixty-first program—a benefit performance for the impresario— that she made her most enduring mark. To the amazement of the audience and most of her fellow artists, the program announced

that she was to play a De Bériot violin concerto. She negotiated this with such consummate musicianship that an encore was demanded. So she sat down at the piano and played a Chopin mazurka. When the delighted audience clamored for more, she thought it best to return to a medium less surprising to them if she was ever to get off the stage. After a whispered conference with Maestro Vianesi, she sang "Ah! non giunge" from *La Sonnambula.* The audience stood and cheered.

Poor Abbey had use of the $20,000 that the benefit program raised. During a season of signal artistic success, in which he had presented nine Italian operas, seven French, two German, and one Austrian—all sung in Italian—and, in Krehbiel's judgment, "the strongest combination of women singers that the city has ever known," he lost substantially more than half a million dollars. There had been two novelties. Ponchielli's *Gioconda* "spoke volumes for the earnestness of the effort which Mr. Abbey was making to give grand opera in a style worthy of the American metropolis"; Krehbiel judged Boito's *Mefistofele* more original, but both singers and public appear to have found it heavy going. The orchestra, if it made a "sad mess" of the *Don Giovanni* Act I finale, played acceptably, and the chorus was "prompt, vigorous and tuneful." Of the dramatic side of these productions the critics had little to say, except for polite comments about the new but conventional stage settings.

Abbey's choice of operas cannot be called adventurous. It reflected the tastes of an era that looked toward the past, at least in cultural matters, and had already grown accustomed to years of Italian opera in New York. Furthermore, the impresario heavily invested his backers' money in the high individual fees of the star system, rather than trying to build a strong ensemble.

But Abbey had firmly established the Metropolitan as a New York institution and a lure to foreign stars. He had given the Academy of Music such competition that "Colonel" Mapleson, after two more downhill seasons, gave up, complaining, "I can't fight Wall Street." Nevertheless, after totting up accounts and paying Abbey his $60,000 guarantee against loss, the Metropolitan directors thanked him and said good-by. While they were not unappreciative of what he had done, their opera house had cost them $1,732,478.71, or more than twice the original estimate, and they were smarting.

The *Daily Graphic* for October 23, 1883, published detail drawings of the splendors that had been unveiled the night before, including décor of the "foyer" later given over to the Metropolitan Opera Club.

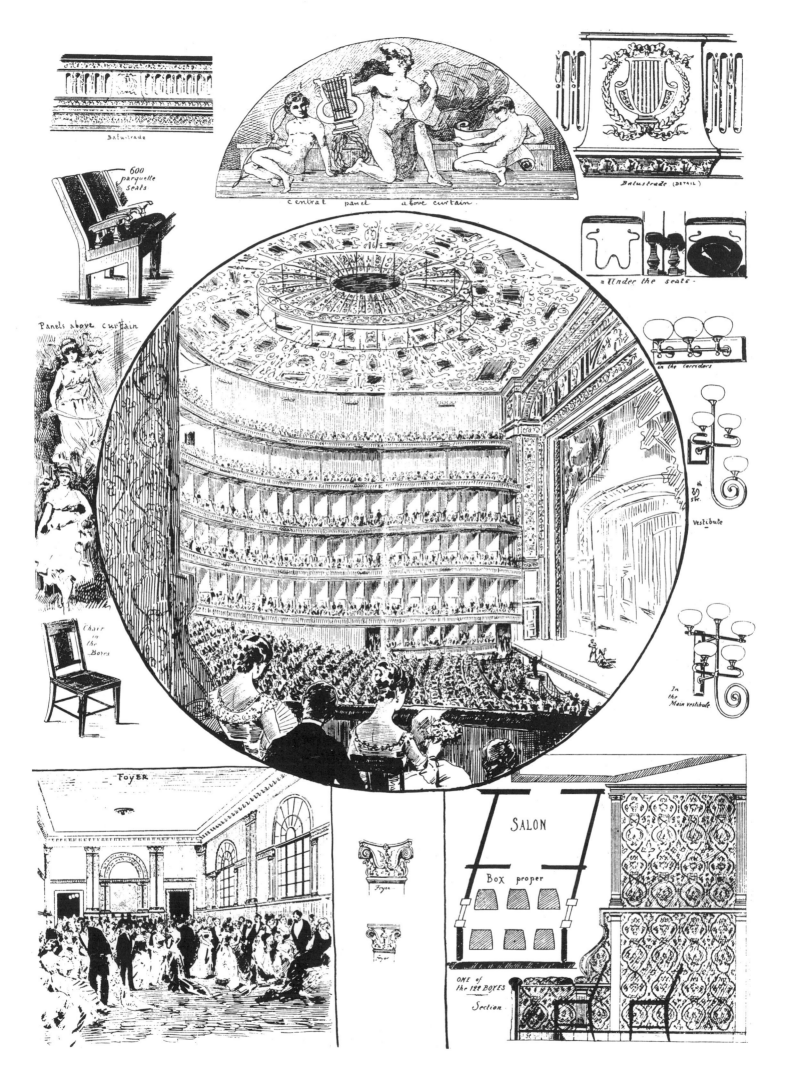

Balustrade

600 parquette seats

central panel above curtain

Balustrade (DETAIL)

Panels above curtain

=Under the seats=

in the corridors

Chair in the Boxes

Vestibule

In the Main vestibule

FOYER

Foyer

Foyer

SALON

Box proper

ONE of the 122 BOXES

Section

Opening-night competition: While the new
Metropolitan echoed to *Faust,* the patrician
Academy of Music (*opposite page*) on Irving
Place was offering Bellini's *Sonnambula*
with the popular Hungarian soprano Etelka
Gerster. Cartoons of the day show why
"Colonel" James Mapleson, impresario of the
Academy, valued her—not to mention Adelina
Patti (*center*) and the other purveyors of vocal
gold shown on this page.

More opening-night competition: Aside from opera, the National Horse Show chose October 22, 1883, to open at the old Madison Square Garden (*opposite page,* "Taking a Hurdle"). Nothing daunted, several fashionable ladies managed to take in two or even all three events; one of them was Mrs. Paran Stevens, shown here not as she made her way around town but in her costume (as Queen Elizabeth) for the Vanderbilt Ball of March 26, 1883.

Dem lieber Freund
Herrn Nahan Franko
zur Erinnerung an unsere
vielen Sarrans.

Marcelin Sembrich

Ornaments of the New York scene: The hit of the Metropolitan's maiden season was Marcella Sembrich (*opposite page*), who made her debut in *Lucia di Lammermoor* on the second night. As on the first night and just about every one that season, the performance was conducted by Auguste Vianesi (*above*), a French-trained Italian with experience at Covent Garden, London. Already established on Broadway was Lillian Russell (*left*), the musical-comedy star familiar as Offenbach's Perichole and Grand Duchess of Gérolstein, who appeared at the Metropolitan Opera House on at least two occasions (not as a member of the Company); Abbey and Grau were her managers.

Shades of Covent Garden: Artists well known in England who graced the beginning and end of the first Metropolitan season included Victor Capoul (*opposite page,* with Paola Marié in a *Périchole* elsewhere), its second Faust; Zelia Trebelli (*left*), its first Azucena and Carmen; Giuseppe del Puente (*below, left*), the opening-night Valentin; and Ellen Terry and Henry Irving, who acted the trial scene of Shakespeare's *Merchant of Venice* at the benefit for impresario Henry E. Abbey that concluded the season.

Deutsche Kunst
1884–1891

It took no more than a season for the first mistake in the Metropolitan's design to become apparent: 122 boxes were too many. For the second season, the top tier was redesigned as the Dress Circle, which had a fashionable status between box and Orchestra seats. In another move that suggested the house was broadening its economic and social base, ticket prices were lowered. Where Henry Abbey had managed, with a seven-dollar top, to lose $600,-000 during the inaugural season, his successor lost only $40,000 by charging from fifty cents (in the Family Circle) to four dollars. Under the new manager, Leopold Damrosch, single seats were nearly always filled, though the boxes were not.

Damrosch had been second choice with the stockholders as a replacement for Abbey. Though highly respected in the New York concert world, and founder of the Oratorio Society, Damrosch was not identified with opera; he had had some operatic experience in his native Germany, but not so much as was customary for an opera manager. Ernest Gye, manager of Covent Garden in London, had been first choice. Negotiations bogged down, however, and the summer of 1884 wore on with the threat of a dark theater confronting the directors. Then Damrosch submitted a proposal to manage a season of German opera. He offered to do so only at the stockholders' risk, but his estimated costs were so much lower than those of the star-studded Abbey season that his proposal was accepted. He went to Europe in late August to secure the services of German artists, many of whom he knew personally. When he returned, with prospects well in hand, news of his appointment came as a surprise to the public at large.

Damrosch's chief passion was Wagner. The German composer, dead only a year, had been both idol and friend to the conductor, who now sought to introduce his works to the New World. Wagner's music was still "modern" in 1884—a period in which conservatism prevailed, in any case in artistic matters. German performing artists had not yet acceded to the star system of the Italians, with its high fees and interpretative license; their musical world was one of discipline and reverence for the score. In the New York of that day, intellectual appreciation counted for little in Italian and French opera; the voice was all. Among Germans, however—and many critics and teachers of music were German, or the descendants of German immigrants—art was taken seriously. Where the Italians conceived of opera as aristocratic entertainment, the Germans thought of it as moral uplift. The difference was thus one of principle to the Germans, and the effects of this split are felt to this day in the condescension shown in certain circles toward non-Wagnerian opera.

A decisive factor in the Metropolitan's acceptance of Damrosch's proposal may have been the assured support it could expect from New York's German population, then numbering 250,000. Operas were to be sung in German, even if the work had been written in Italian (Verdi's *Rigoletto*) or in French (Auber's *Muette de Portici*). After all, a similar convention had been acceptable the first season, when even *Lohengrin* was sung in Italian.

The Damrosch season was successful from the very first. The opening *Tannhäuser* drew an audience of 5,000, a larger number than had attended the grand inaugural of the previous season; many had to be turned away. But the impresario, doing double duty as music director, had not long to enjoy his success. He conducted every performance, and toward the end of the season fell ill of pneumonia and overwork. On February 11, 1885, his twenty-three-year-old son Walter, whom he had briefed from his sickbed, took the baton so that *Tannhäuser,* and *Die Walküre* the following night, would not have to be canceled. "I knew my father was dying," the young man later recalled, "but I knew he would die happier if he was sure the performance took place."

Leopold Damrosch was given a funeral service in the Opera House where he had so quickly and surely established the "music of the future." After his death critics continued to describe the Metropolitan's performance in glowing terms. Certainly the soloists included some of the finest Wagnerian voices of the day. The faithful flocked to hear *Tannhäuser* with Auguste Kraus and Anton Schott, and *Die Walküre* with Amalia Materna, the favorite Brünnhilde at Bayreuth. They heard other German works as well—*Fidelio,* with the intensely dramatic Marianne Brandt, and *Der Freischütz,* with Marie Schröder-Hanfstängl.

The repertory was not all German, however, regardless of the language in which it was sung. Schröder-Hanfstängl, famous in Paris and a pupil of Pauline Viardot-García, was called by W. J. Henderson in the *Times* "one of the few artists of the age in whose style the grace and beauty of the Italian methods are combined with the sincerity and beauty of singers of the German school"; in Act III of Halévy's "morbidly atrocious" *La Juive* she interpolated an aria from Meyerbeer's *Robert le Diable.* She also sang Gilda in *Rigoletto*—a production in which Mme. Brandt, singing the role of Maddalena, interpolated a Spanish popular song in German! The rising tide was Wagnerian intellectualism,

---

Founder of the Metropolitan's German establishment: Leopold Damrosch and his son Walter, who took over the baton as the father lay dying from the exertions of his one season as manager.

THE LOBBY!

V. Gribayédoff

"A First Night at the Metropolitan Opera House": This composite drawing from a New Year's supplement to the *Amusement Bulletin* shows the stylish audience that attended *Lohengrin* on November 30, 1888. Walter Damrosch conducted a cast that included Max Alvary, singing his first Swan Knight at the Opera House, and Katti Bettaque (later Senger-Bettaque) as Elsa.

1. William Steinway
2. Oswald Ottendorfer
3. W. Kurtz
4. Gen. Eckert
5. Collis P. Huntington
6. Walter Damrosch
7. Harry Simms
8. Mrs. Wyatt
9. Elliott T. Shepherd
10. Bill Nye
11. Judge Rufus C. Cowing
12. Charles A. Dana
13. John Jay
14. Mrs. Croly ("Jennie June")
15. Dr. Croly
16. E. Campbell Allison and w
17. George Bliss

THE BOXES!

THE ASTOR BOX

HENRY CLEWS' BOX

C. VANDERBILT'S BOX

18. Mrs. G. Bliss
19. Pierre Lorillard
20. Mrs. Lorillard
21. Miss Catharine Brady
22. Judge Brady
23. Miss May Brady
24. S. L. M. Barlow
25. Jules Montant
26. Gen. Daniel S. Sickles
27. Gen. W. T. Sherman
28. Col. John A. Cockerill
29. Edward S. Stokes
30. Miss Phillips
31. Henry Hilton, Jr.
32. Washington E. Conner
33. Addison S. Cammack
34. General Manager Stanton

35. E. Berry Wall
36. Miss L. Wall
37. Mrs. Frank Leslie
38. Gen. John Cochrane
39. Dr. Fordyce Barker
40. Cashier Max Hirsch
41. Gunning S. Bedford
42. Jean Jacques R. Mayer
43. J. I. C. Clarke
44. Frank Work
45. Joseph Howard, Jr.
46. W. S. Hoyt
47. Dr. Oliver Haight
48. Douglas Robinson
49. Adolph Ladenburg
50. Stanley Mortimer
51. Frederick Bronson

52. F. B. Cutting
53. Romaine C. Nicholl
54. Edmund Knoedler
55. Foxhall Keene
56. J. I. D. Lanier
57. William R. Traver, Jr.
58. Woodbury Kane
59. George Work
60. Lawrence Turmore
61. Thomas Howard
62. Phillip Allen
63. Charles Munn
65. Miss Martha Otis
66. Miss Jeanne Burrowe
67. Mrs. R. L. Clarkson
68, 70. The Rutherford boys
69. William Cuttings, Jr.

71. Miss Bulkley
72. Miss Emily Heckscher
73. Miss Georgie Heckscher
74. Prescott Lawrence
76. The Duke of Marlborough
77. Henry Clews
78. Mrs. Clews
79. The Duchess of Marlborough
80. Lady Manderville
81. Mrs. Burke-Roche
82. John J. Astor, Jr.
83. Miss Mabel Wright
84. Ward McAllister
86. William Astor
87. Mrs. Orme Wilson
88. William K. Vanderbilt
89. Col. Jay

90. Cornelius Vanderbilt
91. Mrs. W. K. Vanderbilt
92. Mrs. Alfred Paget (daughter of Mrs. Paran Stevens)
93. Mrs. Adèle Grant
94. Mrs. Cornelius Vanderbilt
95. Max Alvary
96. Katti Bettaque

but it did not obscure the predilection of an earlier era for singing as such.

The vacancy left by the death of Leopold Damrosch was filled the following season by the Hungarian Anton Seidl, of the Bremen Stadttheater. Only thirty-five, and married a year before to the soprano Auguste Kraus, the imperious Seidl was appointed Metropolitan musical director, sharing the responsibilities with Edmund C. Stanton as manager. Walter Damrosch and his brother Frank alternated as second conductor, and the next season Walter Damrosch held that post alone, sharing the repertory with Seidl.

Seidl, a former secretary and protégé of Wagner, asserted his mastery from the outset. Though the critic Henderson felt it unseemly for a new conductor to take curtain calls so eagerly, he conceded that the *Lohengrin* which opened the 1885–1886 season was "finely managed, the fortissimos being wrought up by well-nigh imperceptible gradations." For him, as for Leopold Damrosch, Wagner was a religion, though he conducted other operas, even *Faust*. A hard taskmaster, Seidl treated the soloists, however renowned, as mere acolytes doing their duty. On one occasion he even disciplined the all-powerful boxholders, stopping the performance until they quieted down. Seidl showed no special cordiality toward Walter Damrosch, who had in fact engaged him, though he entrusted the younger man with a concert performance of *Parsifal* on March 3, 1886—its New York premiere.

Among the Middle European singers Walter Damrosch engaged was Lilli Lehmann, perhaps the most versatile soprano of her era and certainly one of the hardest-working. In America, she said, artistic avenues were open to her that were closed in Europe, where she had been "typed" in florid roles. Though famous for her Wagnerian repertory and later for her performance in Bellini's *Norma,* which she chose to sing when offered an evening for her own benefit, Lehmann made her Metropolitan debut as Carmen. One reviewer found her "comely though severe" and appraised her voice as "powerful and ringing." Her rival was her predecessor at the Metropolitan, Marianne Brandt. Mme. Brandt blamed Lehmann (though other observers blamed that favorite target, the society audience) when, during a *Fidelio* of January 1887, a woman's laughter rang out from the boxes after Brandt, as Leonore, vowed that she had done "nothing" for her liberated husband, Florestan.

A new tenor, Max Alvary—called a "matinee idol of enormous conceit" but praised for his "splendid vigor and freedom"— was one of the male stars imported early in the German era, as was the "musical and dignified" baritone Emil Fischer, the first

Hans Sachs in America and one of the great interpreters of the role. In 1886–1887 came Albert Niemann, who at fifty-seven sang Tristan "with rare intelligence and experience" to Lehmann's Isolde in the American premiere, high point of a season that also brought the first Metropolitan *Aida.* Verdi's work introduced the soprano Theresa Herbert-Förster, who had told Walter Damrosch she would come if the Metropolitan found a place for her intended husband, Victor Herbert; he became a cellist in the orchestra.

The Metropolitan's German management found the house well suited to Wagner, but the dialogue and intimate quality of *Singspiel* in *Fidelio* and *Der Freischütz* tended to become lost in so large an auditorium. The repertory was varied, therefore, with works of the genre of *Les Huguenots* ("a distinct disappointment" under Leopold Damrosch), *William Tell*, *Le Prophète, La Muette de Portici*, and *La Juive.* These gave the "German seasons" a cosmopolitan tone overlooked by many historians, whose abhorrence of the period is as total as the Wagnerians' admiration. But it was Wagner who carried these seasons—an ironic fact in view of the composer's inability during his lifetime to make ends meet at the Bayreuth Festival.

The big money-maker of the second German season was Goldmark's *Queen of Sheba.* Praised for its stageworthy libretto and mounted at a cost of $75,000, it ran a total of fifteen performances—a record unbroken until Rudolf Bing's nineteen *Fledermaus*es of 1950–1951—and helped hold the losses for 1885–1886 to a relatively modest $25,000.

Seidl had to wait two more seasons to realize one of the dreams he had shared with Leopold Damrosch: the first complete *Ring* cycle in America. The critic Krehbiel—who thought *Tannhäuser*'s libretto better than *Tristan*'s because of its "ethical element" but conceded the power of the latter's score in conveying passion—found *Siegfried,* with its strange assortment of characters, even bolder than *Tristan,* and he judged *Götterdämmerung* the most sympathetic of the *Ring* dramas.

The Flying Dutchman opened the 1889–1890 season, and Wagner's nine other major works followed in the space of three months—a tour de force that has not been duplicated, even at Bayreuth. Not until the multiple *Tristan*s of the late 1930's, with Flagstad and Melchior, did Wagnerism again suggest the proportions it attained in Seidl's day. To be sure, the director had leav-

Debutante of the second German season: on the second night (November 25, 1885) Lilli Lehmann, who had come to America to escape type-casting in *bel canto* roles, made her bow as Carmen.

PROGRAMME.

37th Night of the Subscription,

WEDNESDAY, JANUARY 25th, 1888,

FIRST PERFORMANCE IN AMERICA OF

RICHARD WAGNER'S MUSIC - DRAMA,

"DIE GÖTTERDÄMMERUNG."

SIEGFRIED,	Herr NIEMANN
GUNTHER,	Herr ROBINSON
HAGEN,	Herr FISCHER
ALBERICH,	Herr von MILDE
BRÜNNHILDE,	Frl. LEHMANN
GUTRUNE,	Frau SEIDL KRAUS
WOGLINDE,	Frl. TRAUBMANN
WELLGUNDE,	Frl. BRANDT
FLOSSHILDE,	Frl. MEISSLINGER

Vassals and Women of Gunther's Court.

ACT I.—On the Rock of the Valkyries.
  Gibichung Hall on the Rhine.
  On the Rock of the Valkyries.

ACT II.—Border of the Rhine before Gibichung Hall.

ACT. III.—Woody Country on the Rhine.
  Gibichung Hall.
  Burning of Walhall.

Musical Director, Herr ANTON SEIDL.

Stage Manager........ ....THEODORE HABELMANN.
Chorus Master. ....FRANK H. DAMROSCH.

The Knabe Pianos used at the Metropolitan Opera
House and by the Artists of the Company.

The Roosevelt Pipe Organ used.

All the Music Performed at this Opera can be had at
G. Schirmer's 35 Union Square, New York.

"Wagner's Dream at Bayreuth" realized in U.S.: An undated woodcut (*opposite page*), showing Wagner banishing Italian opera, suggests how he must have appeared to Metropolitan boxholders of the nineties. However much they may have deplored the dark stage settings and unrelieved seriousness of Wagner's art, they surely appreciated such an extraordinary dramatic cast as was assembled for the premiere of *Götterdämmerung*. Anton Seidl, Wagner's former secretary (*above*), conducted.

The Ringmaster and his three-*Ring* circus: The elegant figure at left is Edmund C. Stanton, secretary of the Metropolitan Opera-house Company, Ltd., and general manager from 1885 to 1891. In addition to overseeing three *Ring* cycles—the first in America—in 1888–1889, Stanton directed a stable of Central Europe's best singing actors. Shown on the opposite page are Anton Schott as Lohengrin, Max Alvary as Walther von Stolzing, Joseph Beck as Alberich, and Auguste Seidl-Kraus, wife of the conductor, as Eva; on this page are Amalia Materna as Brünnhilde, Emil Fischer as Hans Sachs, Marianne Brandt as Fidès (in *Le Prophète*), and Albert Niemann as Tannhäuser.

ened the heavy diet with Spontini's *Fernand Cortez* (1887–1888), a new production of Meyerbeer's *L'Africaine,* and two new vehicles for the amazing Lilli Lehmann—Verdi's *Ballo in Maschera* and the dramatically pyrotechnical *Norma*—with only a few complaints from the ticket buyers, of whom, the *Times* estimated by January 1891, "the Germans comprise three-fourths."

Boxholders, however, increasingly sought refuge from the brooding music in frivolous conversation, to the indignation of devout Wagnerians. The chairman of the stockholders' entertainment committee was said to have requested Seidl to play the third act of *Die Meistersinger* first, since this was the "only act that had music in it." The management did humor its wealthy patrons to the extent of having the lights turned up during the prison scene of *Fidelio*—with predictable results among the German audience when Florestan exclaimed "God! What darkness here!" When admonitory shushes and glares had no effect in quelling disturbances from the boxes, the directors took the unprecedented step of posting a polite but firm notice in each box.

Further pressed to lighten the fare, Edmund Stanton in 1890–1891 chose a "remedy" that, by pleasing neither faction, hastened the end of the German era at the Metropolitan. He imported a trio of unfamiliar but hardly new operas by a duke (Saxe-Coburg's *Diana von Solange*), a baron (Franchetti's *Asrael*), and a nonentity (Smareglia's *Vasall von Szigeth*). These works were given short shrift, the first being withdrawn after two performances at the petition of three hundred opera-lovers. At the same time the number of Wagner operas in the repertory, and the ranks of the specialists who sang them, were reduced. Opposition to both these moves brought about two difficult decisions. In January 1891 it was announced that the following season, despite an almost certain increase in cost, opera at the Metropolitan would be sung in Italian and French; the remainder of the current season was to be one last, conciliatory orgy of Wagner.

The orgy ended—at the matinee of March 21, 1891—with a performance of *Die Meistersinger.* As Emil Fischer delivered his final apostrophe to "heil'ge deutsche Kunst" (sacred German art), ticket-buying members of the audience, many of whom had become subscribers, pelted the baritone with flowers and cheered him and Seidl until the singer was obliged to say a few words. He said them in English.

In January 1889 *Harper's Weekly* published these drawings to show its readers how the newfangled stage effects for *Das Rheingold* facilitated the gods' entry into Valhalla by way of a rainbow bridge, and the swimming of the Rhinemaidens at the outset.

The end of a symphonic era: By the time Walter Damrosch (*opposite page, top*) was photographed on Fifth Avenue in 1899, walking past Lord & Taylor, the low-priced and highly disciplined art his father had fought for at the Metropolitan was a thing of the past. Its end had been hastened by a trio of second-rate operas—by a duke, a baron, and a nonentity—all of which starred a German tenor named Andreas Dippel, who two decades later would become co-manager of the Metropolitan (with Gatti-Casazza). Meanwhile, conductor Damrosch repaired uptown to lead his New York Symphony at the new Music Hall on Fifty-seventh Street (*left*), whose cornerstone had been laid by its donor, Andrew Carnegie—just behind the pulley in the photograph below. Dippel sang at the opening.

Diamond Horseshoe, Golden Voices
1891–1903

When he built the Metropolitan Opera House in 1883, Josiah Cleaveland Cady went to great pains to make it fireproof. When Henry Abbey and Maurice Grau took over from Edmund Stanton as impresarios in 1891, they went to almost as great pains to insure its flammability. They replaced Cady's cumbersome iron stage supports with wooden posts, to create more space for the storage of tinderlike flats and drops. They emptied the water tank designed to feed Cady's primitive but ingenious sprinkler system, because it froze in winter unless it was heated, which was an expensive nuisance. And in the humid summer of 1892, when they were painting scenery on the Metropolitan stage—whether for an opera or another of their theatrical enterprises is an unresolved question—they chained up Cady's asbestos curtain to allow ventilation. Under such conditions it took only some paint-thinner and a cigarette to gut the house. Abbey and Grau supplied the first, a workman the second.

It was the hottest August 27 ever at Broadway and Fortieth Street, and when firemen finally extinguished the flames the damage amounted to $300,000. Only $60,000 of this was covered by insurance—an amount that the directors had deemed more than enough for a "fireproof" building.

The shareholders of the Metropolitan Opera-house Company, Ltd.—some of them already discouraged at the choice between producing lilting Italian opera at huge losses or thundering German opera at small ones—declined to undertake repairs. Instead, they sold out to a group comprising nineteen of the original stockholders and sixteen newcomers, each of whom bought $30,-000 worth of stock and became the owner of one of thirty-five Parterre boxes, and for $30,000 worth of bonds received a thirty-fifth interest in the real estate. They incorporated as the Metropolitan Opera and Real Estate Company and set about rebuilding the interior from its illustrious ashes.

When the Metropolitan reopened in the fall of 1893, after a year of darkness, the most spectacular change was the installation of electric lights, which, glittering on the jewels in the Parterre boxes where Society now was concentrated, soon caused the "Golden Horseshoe" to be renamed the "Diamond Horseshoe."

The unpopular *baignoire* boxes were gone, replaced by what ultimately proved to be equally unpopular: the Orchestra Circle, whose occupants sat in steeply tiered seats at either side of the

Orchestra, facing one another across the auditorium. They also faced the boxes on either side—now reduced to a total of seventy in two tiers—where the fashionable of the Gay Nineties assembled in a fresh décor of cream, red, and gold and put on quite a performance themselves.

In the season they managed before the fire, Abbey and Grau had delighted Wagner-sated elements of the audience by presenting five new *bel canto* artists in French opera. They had opened the 1891–1892 season with *Roméo et Juliette,* introducing the American soprano Emma Eames, the Polish tenor Jean de Reszke, and his brother Edouard, a bass. Later performances offered Lillian Nordica as a majestic Valentine in *Les Huguenots* and Jean Lassalle, baritone friend of the De Reszke brothers, as Nelusko in *L'Africaine.*

The managers escaped open blame for the blaze, despite angry talk, and in the 1893–1894 season won favor for another bass, Pol Plançon, and two exceptional sopranos, Emma Calvé and Nellie Melba. The volatile Calvé followed her fiery debut as Santuzza with a Carmen that critics pronounced "ideal," while Melba progressed from *Lucia di Lammermoor* ("the finest since Sembrich") to Nedda in the Metropolitan's first *Pagliacci.*

The Metropolitan's first *Nozze di Figaro,* on January 31, 1894, boasted another outstanding cast: Eames, Nordica, Sigrid Arnoldson, Edouard de Reszke, and Mario Ancona. Earlier stars such as Emmy Fursch-Madi, Sofia Scalchi, and Italo Campanini returned to the roster; soon to come, in 1894–1895, were the Italian heroic tenor Francesco Tamagno and Gascon baritone Victor Maurel, both chosen fifteen years before by Verdi for the world premiere of his *Otello.* Maurel was to repeat not only Iago but his original Falstaff, with baritone Giuseppe Campanari leaping "at a single bound" to prominence as Ford.

The success of Abbey and Grau (a third partner, John Schoeffel, never figured actively in the management of the Metropolitan) was remarkable in the light of Abbey's financial catastrophe in the opening season of 1883. Much of the credit was Grau's. Educated as a lawyer in his native Moravia before succumbing to the lure of the theater, he knew where to spend a dollar and where to save a nickel. "Grau will give you a good cigar," his friend Jean de Reszke observed, "but not the match to light it with." His ambivalent approach to finance suited the times. It was an era of extravagant voices, with temperaments and tastes to match. Stars costumed themselves, selected their own roles and took vast liberties with scores, but they were sure-fire box office, and Grau was willing to pay their prices. Importing

---

Lillian Nordica (shown as Aida), born Norton in Farmington, Maine, was one of two Down East divas to brighten the Metropolitan's "golden age"; the other, Emma Eames, opened the 1891 and 1893 seasons.

The hottest August 27 on record: The fire that closed down the Opera House during 1892–1893, shown here as seen from across Seventh Avenue, was caused by a can of paint-thinner (supplied by the management) and a cigarette (supplied by a workman).

Luminaries of the Age of Gold: The Australian soprano Nellie Melba (*opposite page*) opened the 1894–1895 season as Juliette; her rival from Covent Garden days, Emma Eames, had sung the Metropolitan premiere of Gounod's opera three years earlier and also opened the next season, 1893–1894, as Marguerite in *Faust* (*left*). The bass-tenor team on all three occasions were the Polish brothers De Reszke—Edouard (*opposite page, left*, as Méphistophélès) and Jean (as Roméo).

stars who already had international reputations, largely from Covent Garden, he presented names like Ernestine Schumann-Heink, Antonio Scotti, Milka Ternina, Johanna Gadski, Sybil Sanderson, Louise Homer, Marcel Journet, David Bispham, and Fritzi Scheff. They packed the house (in a day before restrictive fire regulations), drawing as many as a thousand standees. On the other hand, Grau had only sixty-five musicians in the pit, at $50 a week each, and the same number of singers in the chorus, at $15 a week. Staging and ensemble were generally appropriate to a theater that had only two telephones and no running water in the dressing rooms.

Born in Brünn (Brno), Austrian Moravia, Grau was multilingual, courtly, sincere but rather remote in manner; he knew his performers as well as he knew his patrons. He loved to play poker, and when he became sole manager of the Metropolitan in 1898–1899 it was to his own cronies (including Frederick Rullman, the publisher of librettos) that he turned for backing, not the men of wealth among the boxholders. Grau managed the difficult step of reorganizing his management with the finesse of a man who played the stock market himself. Abbey's death in October 1896 had ended the three-way partnership, but Grau averted its ruin by offering creditors his own third of the debts.

The reorganization did mean a season (1897–1898) without any opera by the resident company, but Grau maintained the lease. Meanwhile, Walter Damrosch and his partner, Charles A. Ellis, erstwhile manager of the Boston Symphony, rented the house for a five-week guest season. Since leaving the Metropolitan after the German years there, Damrosch and his New York Symphony had been employed at Andrew Carnegie's new Music Hall, later renamed Carnegie Hall, uptown at Fifty-seventh Street.

Because Nellie Melba, who had been "unavailable" to Grau for the 1897–1898 season, was willing to sing for Ellis, who happened to be her personal manager, the Damrosch-Ellis interim visit was a success, aided by the impressive Brünnhilde of Lillian Nordica and the return of several other favorite stars. Indeed, the season did so well Grau declined to release the house for a return engagement the following year. An announcement in the program for Melba's opening *Traviata* of the Damrosch-Ellis season made it clear why: Grau, who spent his sabbatical in London recruiting talent, was ready to announce the return of a resident company to the Metropolitan.

For his first season as sole impresario, Grau announced that he had retained "Mr. Dangerfield, chief scenic designer of Covent Garden," and would bring back Anton Seidl—who had been displaced, along with Stanton, in 1891—to share the podium with

Luigi Mancinelli and Emilio Bevignani. But Seidl died before the season began, so Grau hired Franz Schalk, a Wagner specialist who distinguished that season of 1898–1899 by leading the first uncut *Ring* cycle in the United States. Mancinelli twice conducted his own opera *Ero e Leandro,* to a libretto by Boito, with Eames, Albert Saléza, and Plançon. A novelty of Grau's final season, 1902–1903, was *Der Wald,* by Ethel Smyth, an Englishwoman—though the opera had a German libretto—and the only female composer whose work has been performed at the Metropolitan. "Not worth the labor," wrote the critic Krehbiel, who suggested that private influences had prompted the production.

For a man with one eye on the stars and the other on the balance sheet, Grau introduced a surprising number of significant works to the Metropolitan repertory. *Werther* and *Samson et Dalila* were first mounted under his aegis, as was Mozart's *Zauberflöte*—billed as *Il Flauto Magico* and served up as a *bel canto* attraction. From Italy came three important new scores that remain standards: Verdi's *Falstaff,* Puccini's *Tosca* and *Bohème.* Not to fare so well was Paderewski's *Manru,* whose premiere in 1901 the celebrated composer-pianist-patriot-statesman attended, lurking shyly in the back of his box until his compatriot, Mme. Sembrich, coaxed him onstage to accept a massive floral wreath.

Grau's bequest to the Metropolitan was practical as well as artistic. For all his extravagance of stars, he was able to survive with a five-dollar top ticket price—an increase of only one dollar from the "economical" German years. So efficient was the system he instituted that with the exception of special performances at higher prices, such as the famed all-star *Les Huguenots* with Melba, Nordica, Scalchi, the De Reszkes, Plançon, and Maurel, the price scale went unchanged for eighteen years.

All in all, the Grau tenure was memorable. If prima donnas dictated what parts they would perform (Melba went beyond her depth by attempting the *Siegfried* Brünnhilde), the public delighted in the beauty of their voices. If the spectacle was something less than well-rounded theater, it satisfied the demand of a booming epoch for figures larger than life. And if ever the profusion of golden voices cloyed or the performance onstage lagged, there was always the show in the boxes.

Strong men of the Gay Nineties: J. P. Morgan, seen (*opposite, above*) threatening a photographer, held Box 35 at the very center of the Golden Horseshoe—a fitting position for the Colossus of Wall Street. One of the singers he surely admired was David Bispham (*below,* keeping fit), a Philadelphia baritone who specialized in Wagnerian roles.

Social arbiter of the golden age: Supper parties after the opera or Horse Show, in Delmonico's or at the Waldorf (*opposite page,* the hotel's new ballroom in 1896), emulated the tone set by "Mrs. [William] Astor," the former Caroline Schermerhorn, who reigned as mistress of "The 400." (Portrait by Carolus Duran.)

The Metropolitan Opera House as it looked at
the turn of the century: a pair of rare
photographs showing the old porte-cochère
(*below*) on Broadway, and the auditorium
during intermission in 1899 (*opposite page*),
with the cream-colored walls and red upholstery
that were on view between the fire of 1892
and the new décor of 1903–1908. The garlands
festooning the boxes suggest some sort of gala.

Mainstays of the fourteen-carat soloists: Behind the golden-age stars stood the unsung members of the Company who helped them shine. In his crowded office beneath a staircase, Max Hirsch, box-office chief of the Metropolitan, sat surrounded by the stars' photographs (*opposite page*) as his derbied assistants checked tickets. While members of the corps de ballet rested backstage, tambourines on tables (*left*), ladies of the chorus held a rehearsal in their street clothes in an upstairs hall.

Larger-than-life personalities: Three extremes from the heyday of beautiful singing were the Otello of Francesco Tamagno (dying on the opposite page), who arrived in December 1894; the Ophélie of Emma Calvé (dying below him), first heard in December 1895; and the Falstaff of Victor Maurel (*left*), who introduced Verdi's rogue to North America in February 1895.

Slavic star, Slavic impresario: Milka Ternina,
soprano from Zagreb, sang the title role in the
first Metropolitan *Tosca* (February 4, 1901) a
year after Maurice Grau (*left*) brought her
over to sing Wagner's Elisabeth, Sieglinde,
Senta, and all three Brünnhildes; Beethoven's
Leonore; Mozart's First Lady in the first *Magic
Flute*.

Entr'acte: The Familiar Face

By 1903, when the auditorium of the Metropolitan was redecorated, prevailing notions of luxury had grown more sumptuous. Many felt that the rather subdued elegance of the original 1883 décor was not a proper setting for feminine beauty, gowns, and jewels. The remodeling of 1893, after the fire, had improved this, chiefly by adding the brilliance of electric lights. It remained for John M. Carrère and Thomas Hastings to banish the pale colors and give the Golden Horseshoe the deep richness familiar today.

Both men were graduates of the Ecole des Beaux-Arts, Paris, and had served architectural apprenticeships with the reigning firm of McKim, Mead and White in New York. Now in their early forties, they were on the point of making a number of major contributions to the New York scene: the New York Public Library (which in 1911 was to replace the reservoir a block east of the Metropolitan); the New Theater (a project backed by Otto Kahn and Heinrich Conried, new figures at the Metropolitan); the Frick Mansion on upper Fifth Avenue. And Hastings, after his partner's death, designed a chapel of the Cathedral of St. John the Divine. It is symptomatic of the era's changing taste that the Public Library was to be faced with marble while the Metropolitan stood modestly clad in yellow brick, ornamented only by Romanesque arches and the sculptured stucco trim of Lorenzo Rosario.

The key colors of Carrère's and Hastings' Edwardian baroque interior for the Opera House were maroon and gold, the former on hangings and upholstered seats, the latter on ornate plaster reliefs added to the face of each tier of boxes and galleries. The crowning glory of the house, a massive chandelier in the shape of a sunburst, was hung from the round ceiling panel, which in turn was decorated with a design like an elliptical waffle-iron. Some details were never completed: the medallion-shaped panels directly over the center of the proscenium, for example, remained without the paintings doubtless intended for them. As for the proscenium itself, Carrère and Hastings softened its contours.

The analytical eye could discern many sources in the architects' eclectic achievement, from Versailles to the palaces of the Italian Renaissance, but most audiences have been content simply to bask in the warmth of its color and homogeneous ornament.

If oldtimers in the 1903 audience felt that an age of gold was already past, they needed only to look around them to see it reawakened in the visual splendors of the new Metropolitan.

Though only one of its original four tiers of boxes remains, in other respects the auditorium of the Metropolitan Opera House has looked much the same since 1903, when Carrère and Hastings redesigned it.

COLOR SPREAD:

A triumph of Edwardian elegance: The traditional maroon-and-gold décor was unveiled in 1903, the first gold curtain hung in 1905, the ceiling paintings completed in 1908. The rosettes of electric lights ornamenting each level of the Opera House culminate in a massive sunburst chandelier.

Closeup of the familiar face: Only the denizens of the Family Circle can scrutinize the four oval polychrome paintings of music-making *putti* that embellish the Metropolitan's waffle-grid ceiling. More generally legible are the six names carved into the proscenium—Gluck, Mozart, Beethoven, Verdi, Wagner, and Gounod.

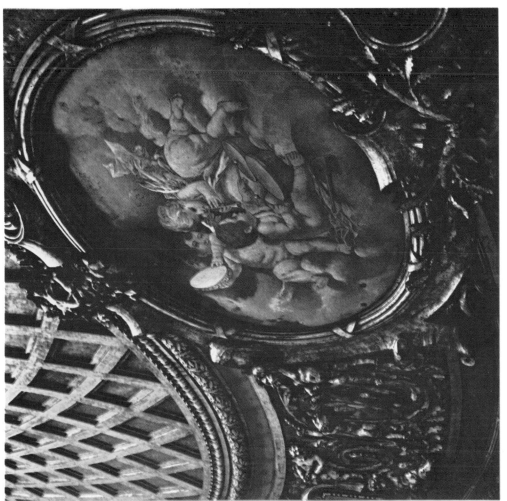

Overlooked in the bustle of intermission: Many small gems of the Metropolitan's décor reveal themselves only to the eye of the photographer, who can choose his angle and arrange his lights without concern for the crowds that throng the Opera House during a performance. Frescoed angels frolic above the Grand Tier foyer; a *fin-de-siècle* fountain is one of two on the Orchestra corridor; Florentine grillwork (*below*) encloses the Fortieth Street elevator.

The Old Lady of Thirty-ninth Street: A comparison of the photograph on the opposite page (*above*) with the one on page 16 shows what has happened to Broadway during the Metropolitan's lifetime. Brash neighbors and a staccato pace have overtaken the "house of princes"; grime has clouded the Seventh Avenue façade, which shows the unequal roof stages added by Gatti in 1909 (left) and 1921 (right) in an effort to compensate for the inadequacies of the stage house and rehearsal space. Sherry's restaurant, too (*below*), harks back to an earlier age. Though its flocked wallpaper and mirrored columns date from 1951, the embossed ceiling and general layout are holdovers from the days when the same space was marked "Assembly Room."

Caruso and Drama
1903–1908

It is ironic that the six composers' names carved into the new Metropolitan proscenium of 1903 failed to include two shortly to be recognized as the giants of twentieth-century opera. *La Bohème* had been heard at the Metropolitan only eight times, *Tosca* nine; *Salome* and *Elektra* were still unwritten. But if some prescient opera-goer missed Puccini and Strauss from the line-up, he would hardly have raised an eyebrow at finding Gounod side by side with Gluck, Mozart, Beethoven, Verdi, and Wagner. The French composer's *Roméo et Juliette* had opened six seasons at the Metropolitan, his *Faust* three. As early as 1897 the *Times* critic W. J. Henderson had dubbed the new theater the *Faustspielhaus.*

New marvels, offstage and on, were unveiled when the 1903–1904 season got under way on November 23 with *Rigoletto,* starring Sembrich, Homer, Scotti, and a new Italian tenor, Enrico Caruso. Behind the scenes was a new general manager, the German Heinrich Conried, and the board of directors had a new member, Otto H. Kahn. The auditorium was resplendent in its new maroon and gold décor by Carrère and Hastings, whose Midas touch had spared only the curtain, which was red; the first gold curtain was not hung until 1905. And there were changes back-stage too, $150,000 worth of them. The flies and borders were given counterbalances, so that scene-changing did not have to rely solely on the stagehands' brawn, and a new stage floor was installed, with traps patterned on those of the Prinzregenten Theater in Munich, which was in turn modeled on the Bayreuth Festspielhaus (a natural derivation, borne out by the placing of Wagner's name among the six on the proscenium). From the same Munich theater came a new technical director, Carl Lautenschläger. The sets he used were painted in Europe.

But if the physical changes at the Metropolitan showed a German influence, the prime news of the day was the new Italian tenor. After his successful if unsensational debut in *Rigoletto*—Caruso was, according to Krehbiel, "musically the finest Duke that New York has heard for a generation . . . but showed many of the tiresome Italian vocal affectations"—he was heard that season in *Aida, Tosca, Pagliacci, Lucia di Lammermoor,* and as the love-sick Nemorino in the Metropolitan's first *Elisir d'Amore,* which earned him praise for his fine flair for comedy. The critics often found Caruso's acting in dramatic roles "bourgeois" or "unstylish,"

but his passionate voice, unique in its solidity and timbre, had its way with most listeners and at the box office. The advent of Caruso made itself felt in the repertory. Ten operas were sung in Italian that season, as against three in French—a proportion quite different from that in the days of Jean de Reszke. With the exception of 1906, when Geraldine Farrar made her debut as Juliette, Caruso sang every opening night for the next seventeen years.

But when the new impresario, Heinrich Conried, was engaged by the Metropolitan he had not even heard of Caruso. The tenor had been placed under option a year earlier by Maurice Grau, and at first Conried was disinclined to honor Grau's terms, which guaranteed Caruso forty performances: he suggested ten instead. (Ultimately Caruso sang twenty-five.) At first Conried had favored the lighter-voiced Alessandro Bonci as a leading tenor, but changed his mind when he heard Caruso on phonograph records. Later Conried played some of these at a press conference announcing his "find."

Conried was a controversial figure, one of the most maligned and most interesting of Metropolitan managers. Born Heinrich Cohn, the son of a weaver in Silesia, he developed a love of the classics as an actor at the Vienna Burgtheater and a love of power as director of various legitimate theaters in Bremen and New York. Unlike Maurice Grau, he was concerned with his public image and that of his staff. He remodeled the executive offices, dressed the Opera House attendants in evening clothes (with silver badges to distinguish them from patrons), made grand appearances in the corridors, and lectured the press, who resented his attempts at manipulating them as well as the fortunes of the Metropolitan.

Conried's appointment had come about through the one man who showed an abiding interest in the Metropolitan during this difficult period and who had the means to make his interest effective. Otto H. Kahn, a partner in the Wall Street banking firm of Kuhn, Loeb and Company, had been proposed for the board of directors by his own senior partner, Jacob Schiff, when the latter was invited to join and felt unable to spare the time. Kahn asked his friend Edward Harriman whether he ought to risk his banking reputation in so frivolous and financially uncertain a field. He was advised to go ahead—if he would treat the opera seriously, as he would any other business. A tireless worker as well as a devoted Maecenas, Kahn filled an eighteen-hour day seven days a week with various interests, and the Metropolitan always ranked high among them. For three decades he poured an

Enrico Caruso, first of a new breed of tenors (shown opposite in his debut role, as the Duke in *Rigoletto*).

New forces on the Metropolitan scene: Otto
H. Kahn (*opposite page, top left*), a musically
enlightened addition to the Board of Directors;
impresario Heinrich Conried (below him),
who favored German drama and Italian realism
over French suggestiveness; and the New York
subway system, which opened October 27,
1904, with Mayor McClellan and guests
boarding flatcars in City Hall station (*left*).
Meanwhile, soubrette Fritzi Scheff (*opposite
page*), who had sung Nedda, Musetta, and
Zerlina under the Grau regime, left the
Metropolitan for stardom in operetta—
especially *Mlle. Modiste* by Victor Herbert,
in which she introduced New York to "Kiss Me
Again."

"Bringing opera theatrically up to date" involved various techniques backstage—the wind machine, "anvils," drum and thunder sheets required for Wagner's *Ring* cycle (*opposite page*); the trucking of ever more solid scenery back and forth from the warehouse (*left,* a sight that has changed only in the design of the truck); and the musical rehearsals demanded by so elaborate a score as *Götterdämmerung* (*below,* conductor Alfred Hertz and assistants in conference with Olive Fremstad and Johanna Gadski on the banks of the Rhine). It also presupposed a realistic dragon for *Siegfried* (*above*).

average of $100,000 a year of his own funds into the Company's upkeep. But in 1903, when he became a member of the new corporation and board which had formed the Conried Metropolitan Opera Company, his power was not yet so absolute nor his aim so clearly set.

Kahn was musically enlightened, having studied three instruments in his youth, but Conried was not. The new manager's predecessor had traded in stars; his successor, Gatti-Casazza, would build repertory. In between, for five seasons, Conried remedied the oversights of the one and prepared the groundwork for the other. He introduced new works, emphasized dramatic values, provided understudies for his stars, avoided repeating any opera within a subscription series, and catered to the whims of the box-holders to the extent of keeping performances of Wagner to a minimum on Monday, the fashionable night. In return he received a handsome salary of $20,000, plus the proceeds of benefit performances, at which the leading singers donated their services in his behalf. Until the end of his career he augmented his income by giving private acting lessons in his office.

As a discoverer of singers, Conried was less effective than other Metropolitan managers. In his first season he introduced Olive Fremstad and Felix Mottl, the latter conducting the *Walküre* in which the incandescent soprano made her debut as Sieglinde. Both artists had been engaged by Grau, however, and Grau had also begun negotiations with Geraldine Farrar, a young American recently risen to stardom in Berlin. The conductor Alfred Hertz had already made his mark under Grau. Conried's one great gift to the podium, Gustav Mahler, did not come until 1907–1908. That season also saw the New York debut of the towering Russian bass Feodor Chaliapin, whose earthy Mefistofele and broad Basilio in *Il Barbiere di Siviglia* so shocked some subscribers and critics that he left in disgust and was not re-engaged for more than a decade. Meanwhile, many important artists unsigned by the Metropolitan—Mary Garden, Maurice Renaud, Luisa Tetrazzini, Giannina Russ, Charles Dalmorès, Mario Sammarco—were creating strong competition at the Manhattan Opera House, under the aegis of Oscar Hammerstein.

In the area of repertory, Conried came closer to justifying his reputation as "a sort of German Belasco." An unqualified success of his initial season was *Parsifal,* the full stage version of which was given its American premiere, at a ten-dollar top, on Christmas Eve, 1903. Wagner had forbidden production of the work outside Bayreuth for fifty years (though a concert version, under Damrosch, had been given at the Metropolitan in 1886), and his heirs

and adherents did their best to stop Conried. The Metropolitan performance won high praise; Richard Aldrich of the *Times* found it "the most perfect production ever made on the American stage" —a tribute as much to Conried's gifts as to the cast, which included Ternina, Burgstaller, and Van Rooy, with Hertz conducting. The impresario also introduced Strauss's *Salome*—banned by the directors, allegedly under pressure from J. P. Morgan and his daughter, Mrs. Herbert Satterlee, after a single performance—as well as *Hänsel und Gretel;* whose composer, Engelbert Humperdinck, was in attendance at its premiere, and Johann Strauss's *Fledermaus.* Conried's repertory included such other new items as Donizetti's *Lucrezia Borgia* and Berlioz's *Damnation of Faust.*

In deference to the rising veristic movement—that "piquant contemplation of adultery, seduction and murder amid the reek and stench of the Italian barnyard," as Krehbiel put it—Conried ventured to open the 1907–1908 season with Cilèa's *Adriana Lecouvreur,* in which the lovely Lina Cavalieri made her debut. Mascagni's *Iris* proved no more durable a repertory item, but Giacomo Puccini's work quickly fared much better. The debonair Tuscan maestro journeyed to New York for the Metropolitan premieres of his *Manon Lescaut* and *Madama Butterfly.* Conried entrusted the staging of *Butterfly* to none other than David Belasco; considered the foremost legitimate-theater director of the period, Belasco was also the author and producer of the play on which the opera had been based.

One of Conried's fondest dreams was the establishment of a national theater in New York, "a people's theater . . . not for the few." Seeing the projected building, which would have all the latest technical facilities, as a possible replacement for the already obsolescent Metropolitan, Kahn fell in step with the plan, and a New Theater was actually built in 1909, after Conried's death, at Sixty-second Street and Central Park West. It was intended to serve also as an adjunct of the opera, as the Opéra Comique does in Paris, and the Metropolitan did stage fourteen lyric works from its lighter repertory in the uptown house. But the theater ran into difficulties. Its architecture was considered pretentious, its acoustics unsatisfactory, and its program of legitimate theater in repertory miscarried; its financial losses were heavy, and the president of the managing organization, Charles Barney, shot himself.

Conried's hope of bringing opera up to date was not a pipe-

"The Bishop of Broadway," David Belasco, dispensed with the famous clerical collar in the privacy of his cluttered studio (*opposite*), where he plotted the staging for *Madama Butterfly* at the Metropolitan (1907).

Competition from Thirty-fourth Street: At the handsome Manhattan Opera House (*opposite page*), which opened in 1906, keen showman Oscar Hammerstein (*above,* with plans for the building) presented opera redolent of the *belle époque* in Paris. His seasons featured stars ignored at the Metropolitan, five blocks uptown —notably Mary Garden (*left*), who had created a sensation at the Opéra Comique in 1900 as Louise and sang the first Mélisande there. She later directed the Chicago Opera.

dream. Even in his day, singing was becoming more robust, acting less genteel; the gaslight era was drawing to a close. A week before the first performance of *Parsifal,* a premiere of another sort took place at Kitty Hawk, North Carolina; the Wright Brothers' first flight heralded a phenomenon that would one day affect repertory and casting schedules in opera houses around the world. Patrons were already making their way to the Metropolitan underground, in the subway system that opened in 1904.

Though Conried often spoke of abolishing the star system, he learned to live with it. He foresaw the day when opera would be given in English and proved his faith in American talent by establishing at the Opera House a modest training program for young singers. When the Company met disaster on tour in San Francisco, during the earthquake and fire of April 18, 1906, Conried took his turn at the Metropolitan switchboard, comforted distraught relatives of Company members, and arranged to refund admission for canceled performances.

The next season sciatic neuritis, helped along by unfriendly criticism, forced him into retirement. On May 21, 1908, Otto Kahn presented to the board a letter he had drafted for them to send Conried, stating that they could no longer agree to add $75,-000 "additional compensation" to the $300,000 he had received in salary, benefits, and profits during his five seasons as manager. The reasons: there was only $30,000 in the bank, not the $130,-000 Conried had said there would be, and the value of the scenery and stage machinery—"so much worn or in such poor taste as not to be of any further use"—did not account for the Company's capital of $200,000, "which has vanished." Conried was further taken to task for having failed, "in spite of the continuous urgings of your board," either to engage Cleofonte Campanini as conductor or to produce modern French operas at the Metropolitan. The board approved the letter, which implied that Conried had furthered Hammerstein's success.

On April 27, 1909, Conried's body lay in state on the Metropolitan stage as mourners overflowed the lobbies and out into the streets. Despite his reprimand by the board, the late impresario may well have taken pride in the fact that of the six composers honored on the ornate new proscenium, four shared his German origins. For the Metropolitan, however, the wave of the future was to come not from the Rhine or the Seine but the Mediterranean.

The new and the old in opera were typified by Feodor Chaliapin (*right*), an "earthy" Mefistofele, and Luisa Tetrazzini (*opposite,* as Philine), whose coloratura graced the Metropolitan only after Conried departed.

Rival versions of *Salome:* The American premiere, staged by Conried in German with the heroine in the intense and superbly sung portrayal of Olive Fremstad (*above,* receiving the head of John the Baptist), was banned after a single performance in 1907. Two years later Oscar Hammerstein revived it in French (*opposite page*), with great success, although Mary Garden's Salome (*left,* with Charles Dalmorès as Herod) was stronger histrionically than vocally. (*Salome* did not return to the Metropolitan Opera House until 1934.)

Rival points of view: In 1907–1908, while Gustav Mahler (*opposite*) was conducting superlative performances of the German-language repertory at the Metropolitan, Cleofonte Campanini (*left*) held forth at the Manhattan Opera House in the fields of French opera and *bel canto*. Heinrich Conried was soon to be taken to task for neglecting these fields.

An opera house is not a home: But this did not deter such a singer as Louise Homer (*opposite,* with husband Sidney and brood) from leading a domestic life concurrently with a career. Another *Hausfrau,* Johanna Gadski, is shown (*left*) at a coaching session in her hotel room; many Metropolitan divas made the Ansonia Hotel (*below,* facing a statue of Giuseppe Verdi) on upper Broadway their home.

The Gods
1908–1921

When the newest of mechanical marvels, the disk phonograph, first startled the musical world, some singers may have feared that the heyday of grand opera was over. If the golden voices of Caruso, Farrar, and others could be had for a song, so to speak, and if, merely by winding a handle, flicking a switch, and guiding a needle into the groove, their best-loved arias could be heard over and over again in the comfort of the living room, why would anyone pay to go to the opera? But lengthening lines at the Metropolitan box office made it clear that a certain breed of music-lover would never be satisfied with a pressed rendition of *Pagliacci* when a live Caruso could be heard onstage. In fact the phonograph turned out to be a boon to opera by greatly enlarging its public.

Another mechanical marvel, the electric elevator, had perhaps a more direct if less wide effect at the box office. When the Opera House was modernized in 1908 two elevators were installed; Family Circle ticket-holders, who until then had struggled step by step to the topmost regions of the house—"for the well-earned privilege," as one of them put it, "of looking *down* on the gods of Valhalla"—were grateful for the lift. Also new that year was the adjustable floor in the orchestra pit, which could now be lowered to accommodate a large Wagnerian orchestra or raised to bring the smaller ensemble of Mozart or Donizetti into more intimate focus.

This new flexibility of movement at the highest and lowest extremities of the auditorium paralleled an even greater change: henceforth the Metropolitan Opera Company was to function as an autonomous producing unit. Through the Opera's first twenty-five years, an ownership corporation had farmed out the responsibilities of producing the operas to an impresario who received a percentage of the season's profits, the rest being divided among the stockholders. In 1908, and for thirty-two seasons thereafter, the operation was divided between two companies: the Metropolitan Opera and Real Estate Company, whose shareholders held boxes but drew no dividends, and the Metropolitan Opera Company, which retained a salaried impresario directly responsible (until 1931) to Otto H. Kahn. Thus the social and artistic responsibilities had been split between ownership and management, and the profits now went into the bank to provide funds for more and better opera.

The new season opened auspiciously on November 16, 1908.

The ceiling had been freshly decorated by Carrère and Hastings, and the new folding seats in the Orchestra, upholstered in bright red and staggered to give a better view of the stage, were filled, as were the boxes, with the best-dressed audience of the year. A silence of anticipation fell as the gold chandeliers were dimmed and a figure ascended the podium and lifted the baton. What followed is history: a performance of *Aida* that has remained unequaled in the annals of New York opera. Emmy Destinn made her American debut in the title role, with Caruso, Louise Homer, Antonio Scotti, and Adamo Didur in the cast. But the real star of the evening was the conductor, Arturo Toscanini, whose first appearance in America signaled a new era at the Metropolitan Opera.

This fiery forty-one-year-old autocrat had come from La Scala with Giulio Gatti-Casazza, the new general manager. Both men had hesitated to accept the offer from the Metropolitan. Neither knew anything about the house at first hand, though Toscanini was impressed that Gustav Mahler of the Vienna Opera had conducted there. Legend has it that Gatti-Casazza received Otto Kahn's telegram offering him the managership of the Metropolitan during a performance at La Scala of Franchetti's *Cristoforo Colombo,* at the moment when Columbus, onstage, sighted America. Gatti booked passage on the *Lusitania,* and, directly upon his arrival, embarked on an exploratory tour of the Metropolitan. He found the house lacking not in grandeur but in backstage space and technical facilities. When he voiced his disappointment to Kahn, he was assured that a new opera house would soon be built —a promise that had to wait fifty-eight years for fulfillment.

Though trained as a naval architect, Gatti-Casazza, with a decade of success at La Scala behind him, knew what he was doing and set about stabilizing the Metropolitan in his own way. He drafted his repertory and cast it shrewdly. He reorganized the chorus and orchestra and ordered the refurbishing of stage sets, many of which sorely needed it. To facilitate rehearsals, in September 1909 Gatti added a roof stage at the northwest corner of the building, at a cost of $25,000. One spur to these measures was an immediate desire to beat Oscar Hammerstein—whose Manhattan Opera House was competing strongly for Metropolitan audiences—at his own game. Where the previous general manager, Heinrich Conried, had felt the stage to be a mission, "acknowledged and respected, side by side with the Church and School, as an uplifting, civilizing, and educational influence," Gatti saw it as Verdi had: as an arena where the audience casts the decisive vote. Certainly this senator's son from Udine, shrewdly eclectic in taste, was the man to out-Hammerstein Hammerstein, aided by Toscanini's energy

---

Along with a new general manager, a new conductor arrived at the Metropolitan to open the 1908–1909 season: Arturo Toscanini, who just a year later presided at the debut of giant tenor Leo Slezak (left).

Friends, Romans, countrymen: Increased crowds
at the Opera house reflected the peak period of
immigration from Europe, 1900–1910. The
heaviest influx was from Italy; many came
steerage (*opposite page, above*) and found
their way to the Metropolitan's Family Circle
(*below*), newly accessible by elevator. Their
countryman Giulio Gatti-Casazza, shown left
with his top-hatted "guardian" Andreas Dippel,
himself arrived on the S.S. *Lusitania*—shortly
to be famous for other reasons.

Opera on cylinder and celluloid: In the first decade of the new century, the early acoustic records were being incised by such singers as the beautiful Lina Cavalieri and her husband, tenor Lucien Muratore, under rather cramped conditions (*opposite page, above*). In the second decade, Hollywood was importing opera singers for silent films (*below,* Goldwyn director Frank H. Crane coaching Mary Garden in *Thais,* 1918); the film capital was also appropriating opera for irreverent purposes (*left,* Charlie Chaplin in a 1915 *Carmen*).

and Kahn's exchequer. In 1910 the enterprising Oscar yielded up his contracts and properties to the Metropolitan for $1,200,000, agreeing to produce no more opera in New York for a decade—though a court order was later required to make him keep his word.

In time, Gatti performed works that Conried had found unsuitable, many of which Hammerstein had done with success: *Boris Godunov, Prince Igor, Pelléas et Mélisande, Thaïs, Louise*. Though he favored these and German works in a cosmopolitan repertory (his own favorite opera was *Die Meistersinger*), Gatti bore out to some extent the prediction of those who had worried at his coming. There could be no denying that the backbone of the repertory was Italian. For while Gatti and Toscanini were taking possession of the New York operatic scene, another Latin invasion was taking place: between 1900 and 1910, when immigration from Europe was at its peak, New York's proportion of Italian-born citizens more than doubled.

During the 1908–1909 season and the one that followed, Toscanini alternated with two other great masters of the podium. Mahler, though tired and near death, conducted a German version of Smetana's *Bartered Bride, Tristan und Isolde* (with Fremstad or Gadski and Burrian), and *Le Nozze di Figaro* (with Eames, Sembrich, Farrar, Scotti, and Didur). The Wagner score had been the vehicle of Mahler's Metropolitan debut the season before and became a bone of contention when Toscanini insisted on conducting it in November 1909. Mozart's comedy was a pendant to the *Don Giovanni* led by Mahler in the season of his debut. Meanwhile Alfred Hertz carried the burden of the Wagnerian cycle and introduced Eugen d'Albert's *Tiefland*.

Among the singers making their first appearance at the Metropolitan during that first Gatti-Toscanini season were Pasquale Amato, who sang Germont in *La Traviata* with an "ample voice of excellent quality," and Frances Alda (later Gatti's wife), who made a less auspicious bow as Gilda in *Rigoletto*. Two important premieres scheduled for the season had to be postponed until 1909–1910: Frederick Shepherd Converse's *Pipe of Desire*, the first American opera given at the Metropolitan, and Tchaikovsky's *Pique Dame*, with Mahler conducting and Leo Slezak and Destinn onstage.

Despite the artistic successes, the company managed to lose over $200,000 in Gatti's first season, a deficit greater than any since the very first year. There were other problems too. Emma Eames and Marcella Sembrich, perhaps feeling their stellar prerogatives threatened, announced that this season would be their

last. Sembrich's gala farewell on February 6, 1909, the twenty-fifth anniversary of her Metropolitan debut, featured a series of excerpts from the soprano's favorite repertory; Farrar, Scotti, and Amato paid her homage by taking *comprimario* roles in the first act of *La Traviata*. A week later, Eames bowed out quietly as Tosca.

Where Grau had indulged his veterans and Conried had assured the leading artists a monopoly over certain roles, Gatti made it plain from the start that he and Toscanini would make the decisions as to which singer would perform what role and when. Perhaps fearing more than the usual artistic rebellions, the directors had, without Gatti's knowledge, appointed an "administrative manager," Andreas Dippel, to act as a safeguard against the Latins. Dippel had proved his worth to the Company as a tenor, and at first many artists, because they knew him, preferred him to Gatti. (Dippel's aspirations had a precedent in those of Max Alvary—who had sparred with Anton Seidl over who was to be boss at rehearsals—and of another Wagnerian tenor, Anton Schott, who competed with Conried for the post of general manager.) During the 1910–1911 season, friction between the two men reached such a pitch that Kahn considered engaging either Oscar Hammerstein or Walter Damrosch to replace Gatti. He eventually resolved the problem by making Dippel manager of the Chicago-Philadelphia Opera, a company also backed by Kahn. Once again all became moderately quiet on the Metropolitan front.

In view of the traditional harassments of theater management, it is fortunate that the new general manager enjoyed a reticent, persevering temperament and a good measure of luck. For seven seasons Gatti-Casazza had the services of Toscanini, for thirteen those of Caruso, for fourteen those of Farrar (who with Caruso formed the "strongest box-office combine in operatic history"). With these artists he set the standards that spelled "Metropolitan Opera" to the rest of the world.

Though Toscanini followed in the wake of such giants as Anton Seidl and Leopold Damrosch, his first *Götterdämmerung* at the Metropolitan was judged worthy of Bayreuth, and German-oriented operaphiles, openly apprehensive about an Italian in the pit, were both relieved and impressed. The Maestro was not successful in establishing such Italian novelties as Puccini's first opera, *Le Villi*, and *La Wally* (written by his close friend Alfredo Cata-

---

Frieda Hempel as a discreetly seated (not recumbent) Marschallin, Margaret Ober as a discreetly jacketed Octavian (*opposite*) in the American premiere of *Der Rosenkavalier*, December 9, 1913.

Visitors to the Golden West: Music publisher Tito Ricordi, Puccini's son Antonio, and the composer came to the United States for the Metropolitan's first world premiere, that of *La Fanciulla del West* on December 10, 1910. The performance, staged by Belasco and conducted by Toscanini, starred Caruso as Dick Johnson, Emmy Destinn as Minnie (here rescuing Johnson from hanging), and Pasquale Amato (pointing) as Sheriff Jack Rance.

The second of the Metropolitan's twenty-five world premieres was Engelbert Humperdinck's *Königskinder* on December 28, 1910, when the cast included Geraldine Farrar, as the Goose Girl, and a large flock of geese.

Boris Godunov arrives in America: The last act of Moussorgsky's opera at the Metropolitan on March 19, 1913, with Angelo Bada as Shuisky and Adamo Didur as the Czar (Toscanini conducting). Gatti considered it his highest achievement.

Gatti emphasized vehicles for high-powered stars, among them Geraldine Farrar and Pasquale Amato, who are seen (*opposite page*) as Caterina Hübscher and Napoleon in the world premiere of Giordano's *Mme. Sans-Gêne,* 1915. At left, Amato is shown throttling Angelo Bada in the American premiere of Zandonai's *Francesca da Rimini;* the American premiere of *L'Amore dei Tre Re* featured Edoardo Ferrari-Fontana as Avito, Lucrezia Bori as Fiora (*below*).

lani), but he accomplished a feat not duplicated until the 1960's—that of making Verdi's *Falstaff* a critical and popular success. In 1910 the Company was considered ready for a tour abroad and was booked for a brief season at the Théâtre du Châtelet in Paris. Debussy, who attended one of the rehearsals for the opening *Aida,* remarked to Toscanini, "I never thought it could sound so beautiful. This is my first intimation of the real genius of Verdi."

Not all the works Toscanini introduced stayed in the repertory, but his average was high. Puccini's *Fanciulla del West,* based on David Belasco's play *The Girl of the Golden West,* was a great success at the outset but has rarely been revived at the Metropolitan; a notable revival was that of 1961–1962. The premiere—on December 10, 1910, with Caruso, Destinn, and Amato—marked the Metropolitan's bid to compete with major European houses in the production of new works. It was the Company's first world premiere: Puccini attended, Toscanini conducted, and the audience, one of the most distinguished ever assembled in the house, paid ten dollars apiece for Orchestra seats. This was double the usual price. "Nothing better from a vocal and dramatic standpoint has ever taken place on the operatic stage," one critic wrote. "No tenor living could have sung the music of Johnson with such tonal beauty, vigor and finish as did Caruso. Destinn, as Minnie, proved a surprise: her creation of the part is one of the finest achievements in her career."

That same season Toscanini led Caruso, Fremstad, and Amato in Gluck's *Armide,* a sequel to the previous year's *Orfeo ed Euridice* and a *succès d'estime.* In the same category as *La Fanciulla del West* was Montemezzi's *Amore dei Tre Re* (1913–1914), one of the last Italian veristic operas to enjoy currency; Weber's *Euryanthe* (1914–1915) was artistically and commercially on a par with *Armide.* A work such as Giordano's *Madame Sans-Gêne* was carried mainly by the superb voice and engaging personality of Geraldine Farrar, Wolf-Ferrari's *Donne Curiose* by the presence of the composer. A success of 1912–1913 was *Boris Godunov,* conducted by Toscanini, with Adamo Didur, Louise Homer, and Paul Althouse. With Chaliapin in the title role, the opera proved one of the greatest hits of Gatti's regime. It was kept in the repertory for seventeen consecutive seasons.

Toscanini made no farewell appearance at the Metropolitan. After the performance of Mascagni's *Iris* on April 14, 1915, he simply departed, never to conduct opera there again. The Maestro had been unhappy about cast substitutions, which in a popular opera such as *Carmen* were visited on him with increasing frequency and sometimes at the last moment. Opposed to humoring the artists, he once told a soprano succinctly, "There are no stars on this stage, madame, only in heaven." Conducting *Aida* on tour, he was incensed to find a Chicago band onstage in place of the group he had rehearsed, which had been left behind for budgetary reasons. In 1915, with war already raging in Europe, Toscanini had further motives for returning to Italy; some were patriotic (the official explanation offered by Gatti), others personal.

Behind Toscanini's dissatisfaction were hard economic facts: the Metropolitan, which had shown the substantial profit of $66,609 from its 1913–1914 season, showed only $1,765 the following year. Since ticket prices had been raised in 1911–1912, a further hike was out of the question, and there was talk of economizing on rehearsals. Toscanini told Kahn, "Good opera is not supposed to make money. It is supposed to lose." But Kahn, who functioned without much help from his board and preferred it that way, was unwilling to risk unpopular or rash courses of action, particularly where fiscal policy was concerned.

Though it was impossible to replace Toscanini, with characteristic luck Gatti-Casazza did find an exceptionally fine conductor in Artur Bodanzky. He came to the Metropolitan for the 1915–1916 season and stayed with the company for nearly twenty-five years, specializing in the German repertory Toscanini, out of deference to Mahler and Hertz, had rarely conducted. In the Italian wing several new conductors had now appeared—Giorgio Polacco, Gennaro Papi, Vincenzo Bellezza, Roberto Moranzoni—and in the French wing Pierre Monteux, who introduced Rabaud's *Marouf* in 1917–1918. Shortly thereafter Monteux left to replace that composer as conductor of the Boston Symphony. Albert Wolff of the Opéra Comique in Paris also joined the Metropolitan to lead the world premiere of his own *Oiseau Bleu,* based on Maeterlinck's *Blue Bird.*

A season earlier, in 1916, a Spanish opera—Enrique Granados' *Goyescas*—was introduced. It was well received, but the composer died soon afterward when the Germans torpedoed the *Sussex,* on which Granados was a passenger. After the United States entered the war, German operas were frowned upon even more than dachshunds, and they were not restored to the repertory until the 1920's.

The Italian wing sustained another loss after Toscanini's departure when Lucrezia Bori withdrew. Bori had been a leading

The first Metropolitan performance of Verdi's *Forza del Destino* atoned for its tardiness (half a century) by means of a cast that included Caruso and Ponselle, shown with Jose Mardones in the last scene.

Varied reactions to World War I: After President Wilson had called for U.S. participation, Ernestine Schumann-Heink sold Liberty Bonds on the steps of New York's Sub-Treasury Building in May 1918 (*opposite*) and returned to the Opera House in 1926, singing there until 1932. Arturo Toscanini had long since returned to Italy, where he led an army band (*below*).

Architects' field day: The year 1909 saw the completion of two unique buildings in New York. On Madison Square rose the Metropolitan Life Insurance tower (*opposite page*), patterned after the Campanile of St. Mark's in Venice; hard by it stood Stanford White's old Madison Square Garden, patterned after the Giralda Tower of Seville Cathedral. Millionaire Harry Thaw had shot White to death in his own roof garden. Two miles to the northwest, the New Theater finally opened (*left,* under its later name); patterned by Carrère and Hastings upon the German court theaters beloved by Heinrich Conried, it had been carried to completion by Conried's successor—with considerable help from Otto Kahn. (*Below,* opening-night audience at the 1916 Diaghilev season there.)

soprano at the Metropolitan since her New York debut, on November 11, 1912, in *Manon Lescaut.* Suffering from a throat ailment, she was not to return to the Company until six years later. But then, after a successful operation, she repeated her earlier triumphs. During Bori's absence, Metropolitan audiences were introduced to several important new singers. Claudia Muzio, whose father had been Metropolitan stage manager under Grau, made her debut as Tosca on December 4, 1916, and quickly established herself, as did Florence Easton, who first sang at the Metropolitan on December 7, 1917, as Santuzza. These two new prima donnas (Muzio in *Il Tabarro* and Easton in *Gianni Schicchi*), together with Farrar (in *Suor Angelica*), helped make the world premiere of Puccini's *Trittico* on December 14, 1918, another glamorous evening, and one of Gatti's triumphs of showmanship. Muzio remained with the Metropolitan only until 1921–1922, when she left to sing with the Chicago and San Francisco companies, but Easton stayed on to fill many roles, among them Saint Elizabeth in Liszt's oratorio of the same name, which replaced *Parsifal* in the repertory during the war years.

Operas of the *bel canto* school (*I Puritani, La Fille du Régiment, L'Italiana in Algerì*) were tentatively revived. But the most auspicious event (which followed the Armistice by a few days and thus caught the audience in a particularly happy frame of mind) was the debut, on November 15, 1918, of the young American soprano Rosa Ponselle. With a poise that concealed her **fright**, Ponselle shared stage honors with Caruso in the Metropolitan's first performance of Verdi's *Forza del Destino.* The next day James G. Huneker wrote in *The New York Times,* "She possesses a voice of natural beauty that may prove a gold mine, with its luscious lower and middle tones, dark, rich and ductile." When Ponselle went on during the same season to sing such diverse roles as Rezia in Weber's *Oberon* and Carmelita in Joseph Breil's *Legend,* it was plain that the Metropolitan had one of its greatest finds. Thereafter, and for almost twenty years, Ponselle was to remain the Company's leading dramatic soprano.

Breil's work was given on a triple bill with two other American operas: *The Temple Dancer,* by John Adam Hugo, and Charles Wakefield Cadman's *Shanewis.* Aside from the apparent influence of Puccini's triple bill, this arrangement showed Gatti-Casazza's opinion that American composers should be introduced by one-act works. That he cast the second with Easton, the third with Sophie Braslau, shows that he meant to do his best by them, as he did with Victor Herbert's *Madeleine,* sung by Frances Alda in 1913–1914. Two other novelties, Henry Hadley's *Cleopatra's*

Night (with Alda, January 31, 1920) and Riccardo Pick-Mangiagalli's ballet *Il Carillon Magico* (with Rosina Galli, December 2, 1920), rode on the coattails of the temporarily sundered "desperate twins" *Cavalleria Rusticana* and *Pagliacci.* Novelty, however, was not the order of the day. The Pax Romana of the Gatti regime relied on established values and commodities for its endurance. Farrar's Thais and Louise were inevitably compared with the earlier impersonations of inimitable Mary Garden, but the Farrar magic never worked more potently than in Leoncavallo's *Zazà,* helped along by David Belasco's stage direction, in 1919–1920.

Caruso's own popularity remained immense. On March 22, 1919, he was honored with a program for the benefit of the Company's Emergency Fund, and later the New York City Police Commissioner presented him with a flag in commemoration of his twenty-fifth year on the operatic stage. Tragedy was soon to follow, however; on December 11, 1920, in Brooklyn a hemorrhage obliged the tenor to stop after the first act of *L'Elisir d'Amore.* On December 13 Caruso heroically returned to the Metropolitan to sing *Forza,* and three days later Samson, only to be injured onstage when a piece of scenery fell on him in the Temple Scene. This did not prevent him from reappearing on Christmas Eve to sing one of his favorite roles, Eléazar in *La Juive,* the opera with which he had inaugurated the 1920–1921 season. The New York *Sun* reported that "Mr. Caruso was once more himself." No one suspected that this would be his last performance. The illness that followed, variously described in the press as lumbago or a wrenched side, was in fact acute pleurisy, and complications caused his death the following summer in Naples, at the age of forty-eight.

During his 18 seasons and 607 appearances at the Metropolitan, Caruso had grown from a promising lyric tenor to a versatile and convincing dramatic figure. Though he never learned to read music—a failing for which his first mentor, Toscanini, took him sorely to task—he was able to memorize over fifty roles, a number of them in contemporary works heard only a few times. In character he was no longer a boyish prankster but the Company's warm and generous mainstay. Indeed, to many Caruso seemed almost the *raison d'être* of opera in New York, and his name on the label of thousands of phonograph records had become the hallmark of opera throughout the world.

When Enrico Caruso was photographed stepping out of his car in 1919, his face already seemed to foreshadow the tragedy that would be enacted two years later, when death struck him down in the prime of life.

Entr'acte:

Beaux Arts

Stage designers today are such a glamorous and highly paid lot that it is hard to realize they were once regarded merely as artisans. In fact only one scenic artist who worked at the Metropolitan before 1910 is remembered by name, and he was actually a copyist: Homer Evans, who duplicated the sets from the Paris Opéra for the American premiere of Louis Reyer's *Salammbô*. Though this was the costliest production in Maurice Grau's twelve-year regime, the opera was performed only twice after its debut on March 20, 1901. Evans' efforts were almost unprecedented; as a rule the painted backgrounds against which the singers moved were sufficiently nondescript to be used for several different operas, and the costuming was equally undistinguished and haphazard. Under the star system the divas often dictated the staging.

With the advent of Gatti-Casazza and Toscanini, genius at last began to illuminate the depths of the stage as well as the apron and podium. Gluck's *Orfeo ed Euridice,* added to the repertory during Toscanini's second season, had sets by Pierre Puvis de Chavannes, "best of the French muralists since [his teacher] Delacroix." Puvis was also commissioned to design the new *Armide* that opened the following season. Mariano Fortuny, a "one-time friend of Wagner" whose name still graces a Madison Avenue atelier, created a new *Tristan und Isolde* in 1909–1910; but by far the most notable achievements before World War I were the sets created by Alexandre Benois for *Boris Godunov.* Originally designed in collaboration with Serge Golovine for the Diaghilev company in Paris, the sets survived at the Metropolitan from 1912 to be repainted in the 1930's.

Sergei Diaghilev's policy of employing fine artists to design and dress his productions had as electrifying an effect on stage design as his stars had on the dance. When Anna Pavlova and Mikhail Mordkin made their debut, with the resident *corps de ballet,* in *Coppélia* (following a performance of Massenet's *Werther*), the audience was spellbound. Traditionally operagoers have always been cool to ballet, and certainly in the early Metropolitan productions little attempt had been made to win them over. Malvina Cavalazzi was the only notable ballerina seen at the Opera House before 1910, but the new Gatti regime, aided by Pavlova and Mordkin, at first showed signs of reversing the trend. Between 1910 and 1914 Lucia (Cia) Fornaroli (later Toscanini's daughter-in-law) served the Company as prima ballerina, to be fol-

Anna Pavlova, seen here in *Dragonfly* about 1915, danced many times at the Metropolitan Opera House but made her debut as a member of the Company on February 28, 1910—following a performance of *Werther*!

Stars of the Metropolitan Opera Ballet: Mikhail Mordkin, Pavlova's partner (shown opposite in his famous Arrow Dance); Lucia Fornaroli (*left*), prima ballerina 1910–1912; her successors Adeline Genée (*opposite, above*) and Rosina Galli (*opposite, below,* as the Queen in *Le Coq d'Or*); Adolph Bolm.

lowed by Rosina Galli. The latter eventually married the general manager and stayed on until Gatti left, over her protests, in 1935 Until the 1930's the dancer most memorable to opera audiences (after Pavlova's pioneer tours) was Vaslav Nijinsky, who made his American debut at the Metropolitan on April 12, 1916, with the Ballets Russes in *Le Spectre de la Rose* and *Petrouchka.*

That Nijinsky appeared at the Metropolitan at all was a miracle. The spring ballet season in which his appearance took place had been included in the Metropolitan subscription series at Otto Kahn's behest. Gatti was reluctant, as well he might have been, for the flash success of the Ballets Russes visit soon gave rise to rumors that Kahn meant to retain Diaghilev, who had managed opera in Europe since 1909, as general manager in Gatti's stead. (Fortunately for Gatti's security, Diaghilev so detested America that he refused to return even for the second season in 1917.) The Ballets Russes opened at the New Theater, where lighter productions from the Metropolitan's repertory were often introduced, and at once the Company ran into trouble. Diaghilev, who told friends he had come to America only for the money, announced at the last minute that his stars would not appear. Nijinsky (whom Diaghilev had fired, in any case, for getting married) was trapped in Europe by the war; Michel Fokine was in the Russian army; Tamara Karsavina was pregnant. Kahn and Henry Russell, his lieutenant, set about getting Nijinsky out of Europe and back into the Company; they succeeded, but apparently only through the intercession of the Austrian emperor, Franz Josef. The composer Igor Stravinsky detained the dancer in Switzerland, demanding money from those ballets for which his music had been used, and when Nijinsky finally arrived in New York he countered by refusing to dance until Diaghilev paid *him.*

Kahn managed to placate Nijinsky, and the moment the dancer leaped onstage from the wings, all such crises were forgotten. For the remainder of the four-week engagement New York audiences marveled at his incredible dancing, and at the impressive *mise en scène* of such artists as Benois (*Petrouchka*), Leon Bakst (*Schéhérazade, Thamar, Spectre*), Nicholas Roerich (*Prince Igor*), and Nathalie Gontcharova (*Firebird*). The first spring ballet season was profitable, but when the Ballets Russes returned the next year, under the "management" of Nijinsky, they lost $300,000 on tour—a sum Kahn charged to the Metropolitan.

In the 1917–1918 season, as if to show that the Metropolitan had been put on its mettle by the Diaghilev troupe, a trio of distinguished artists began to make their contribution. Joseph Urban's *Faust* was the first of fifty Metropolitan productions he

designed. Urban was the semi-official artist of Gatti and Kahn until 1933, and his *Elektra* lasted the life of the Opera House. Willy Pogany's *Coq d'Or* remained one of the Metropolitan's handsomest sights for a quarter of a century, and later he limned a vivid *Italiana in Algeri.* A young American, Norman Bel Geddes, designed productions of three American works in as many seasons: Charles Wakefield Cadman's *Shanewis,* Joseph Breil's *Legend,* Henry Hadley's *Cleopatra's Night. Shanewis,* a tale of an Oklahoma Indian girl's abortive romance with a paleface, shared a bill with an original ballet, *Dance in the Place Congo* (music by Henry F. Gilbert, choreography by Ottokar Bartik, sets by James Fox). The following season Boris Anisfeld brought a "blazing brush" to the design of Xavier Leroux's *Reine Fiammette*; unfortunately the work did not endure in the repertory, nor did Anisfeld's later assignments, Wolff's *Oiseau Bleu* and Boito's *Mefistofele.* Probably the only singer who also designed scenery for the Metropolitan was Victor Maurel, who at seventy did the sketches for Gounod's *Mireille,* which came and went during 1918–1919.

The Metropolitan's own production of *Petrouchka* was one of the successes of that 1918–1919 season; Pierre Monteux conducted (as Ernest Ansermet had done for the Diaghilev version), Adolph Bolm danced the title role and Galli the Ballerina. Stravinsky himself was present when *Petrouchka* was revived in 1924–1925, with the same principal dancers, Serafin conducting and Serge Soudeikine's stage design replacing John Wenger's. Two other ballets were offered by the regular company: in 1920–1921 *Il Carillon Magico* (Pick-Mangiagalli) followed *L'Amore dei Tre Re,* and in 1926–1927 *La Giara* (Casella) brightened a stage just darkened by the death of Madama Butterfly.

Italy and France may have had the edge in the operatic and ballet repertory during the Gatti years, but American designers came into their own. Three rose to prominence during Gatti's last decade: Robert Edmond Jones, Jo Mielziner, and Donald Oenslager. Jones's dynamism was applied to both the choreographic plan and the scenic designs for the ballet *Skyscrapers,* with a jazzy score by John Alden Carpenter (1925–1926); Mielziner's theatrical flair was evident in his designs for the O'Neill-Gruenberg *Emperor Jones*; Oenslager's resourcefulness won him the assignment of *Salome* in 1933–1934. These men paved the way for the achievements under Johnson and Bing.

Sergei Diaghilev, the great dance impresario whose Ballets Russes appeared as part of the Metropolitan subscription season 1915–1916, shown with Alfred F. Seligsberg (*right*), the Opera's legal counsel.

Nijinsky as the Opera House saw him: The star dancer in the death scene of *Petrouchka* (with Orloff and Karsavina) and in *Le Spectre de la Rose* (*left*). He performed both roles at his American debut at the Metropolitan, 1916.

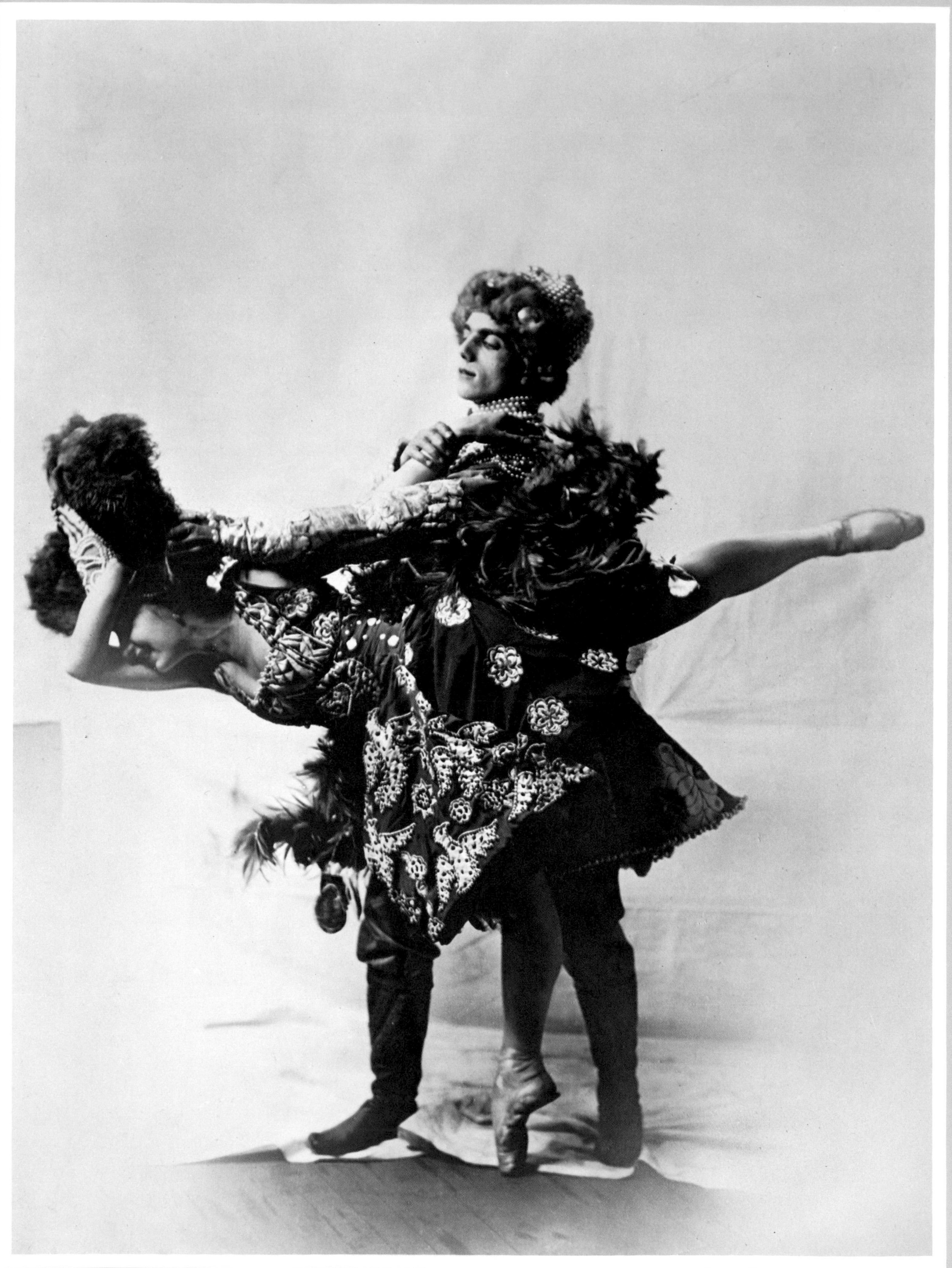

Firebird, prince, and ogre: Leonid Massine, who danced in Stravinsky's ballet during the 1916 spring season, seen opposite with Zenia Maklezowa at a Century Theater performance. Left, Enrico Cecchetti, veteran of Diaghilev's troupe and mentor of Pavlova and Nijinsky.

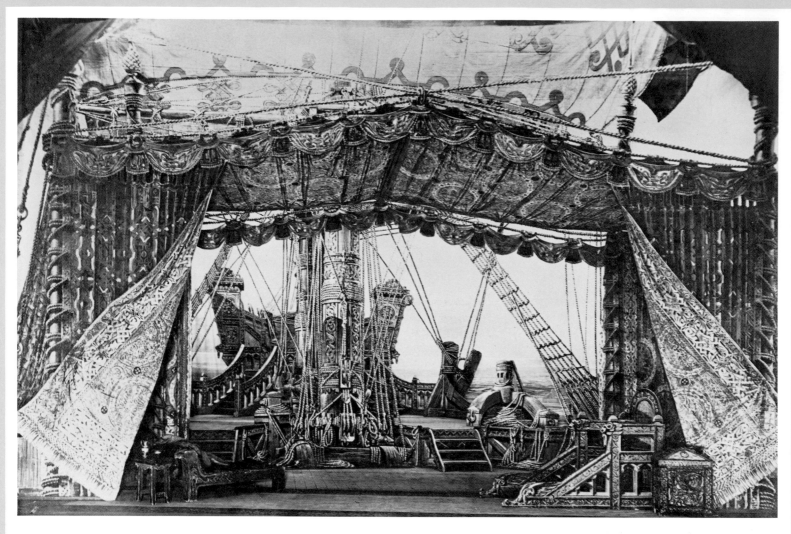

Extremes in stage décor: The first "name" designers to work at the Metropolitan were Mariano Fortuny, whose *Tristan und Isolde* deck scene (*opposite page, above*) was unveiled in 1909, and Puvis de Chavannes, creator of *Armide's* enchanted castle (*below*) in 1910. A distinguished American, Robert Edmond Jones, introduced another kind of look with his design for the ballet *Skyscrapers* (1926).

American opera on its way: Converse's *Pipe of Desire* (*opposite, above*) was the first (March 18, 1910), with Clarence Whitehill, Louise Homer, and others hampered by what one critic called a "hopeless text"; two years later Homer also starred in Parker's *Mona* (*below*, with Riccardo Martin, Rita Fornia, and Albert Reiss), a full-length opera set in Gaul rather than Arcady. *Cleopatra's Night* (January 31, 1920), by Henry Hadley, boasted décor by Norman Bel Geddes but little else of lasting interest; at left is Frances Alda in the title role, dallying with Orville Harrold as Meïamoun.

The Urban point of view: "A Rabelaisian gentleman from Vienna," Joseph Urban brought to the Metropolitan the concept of unified, total theater initiated by Adolphe Appia and others. His training as an architect is suggested by his settings for *La Vestale* (1925, *opposite, above*) and the *Don Carlo* prison (1920); all told, Urban created fifty productions between 1917 and 1933.

Midstream and Full Sail
1921–1929

After the loss of Caruso, the Metropolitan's immediate concern was to hold a saddened, restive audience. The Company needed a new lodestar, and though Gatti-Casazza found several candidates in the 1921–1922 season, none was of the magnitude of the Neapolitan. Caruso's three most popular tenor successors were Beniamino Gigli, who had made his first appearance at the Metropolitan a month before Caruso's last; Giovanni Martinelli, who had joined the Company in 1913; and Giacomo Lauri-Volpi. The first two sang at the memorial matinee concert on December 27, 1921, when a gilded bust of Caruso by Onorio Ruotolo was presented to the Metropolitan by the tenor's widow and placed in the Fortieth Street lobby. It was more than a tribute to a great artist; it was an altar for a long line of singers who, by imitating the passion and volume that had come naturally to him, sought to emulate his success. The three tenor successors, however, sensibly pointed out that there could be only one Caruso.

The first debut of 1921–1922 was that of Amelita Galli-Curci, who opened the season as Violetta in Urban's extravagant new production of *Traviata*. The coloratura was known through records, and New Yorkers had applauded her vociferously with the visiting Chicago Opera Company, but her "pleasing" performance that night was met with reserved enthusiasm. Gigli, who sang Alfredo, was praised for a voice of "really fine quality" but taxed for his disposition to "sing to the audience . . . and cultivate the high note."

Gatti had the highest hopes for his new importation from Vienna's Hofoper, Maria Jeritza, and during the first week of the new season—on Saturday afternoon, November 19—the radiant soprano stepped confidently into the New York limelight in *Die Tote Stadt*. The opera was a pessimistic work by the young Viennese prodigy Erich Wolfgang Korngold (who ended his days in Hollywood, composing for films), but audiences found it "an exhilarating adventure simply to watch the prima donna." They did so again in a memorable *Tosca* on December 1. In the second act, breaking with all tradition, she allowed Scarpia to push her to the floor, where she remained prone for her aria "Vissi d'arte." Deems Taylor's quip, "She scooped to conquer," merely added to the legend of the performance. Tenor Aureliano Pertile's debut in the same production went almost unnoticed, but Jeritza received the greatest ovation Gatti said he had ever heard.

Replacement for the irreplaceable: The first post-Caruso opening night (November 14, 1921) offered Amelita Galli-Curci in the role of Violetta in *La Traviata*.

In quick, spectacular succession, audiences were to see the triumphant return of Feodor Chaliapin—long urged upon Gatti by Otto Kahn—in a performance of *Boris Godunov* "heartbreaking in its pathos"; the debut of Italian baritone Titta Ruffo, who brought his big and usually dramatic voice to a surprisingly "gay and infectious" *Barber of Seville*; and the premiere of Mozart's *Così Fan Tutte,* which had waited 132 years for a New York hearing. The Mozart opera, in Urban's stage-within-a-stage production modeled after the Munich Residenz revival, made its mark, though Aldrich noted in the *Times* that "it cannot be ranked with the greatest masterpieces of the composer." The role of Fiordiligi was sung by Florence Easton, the Company's most versatile soprano since Lilli Lehmann.

Less noteworthy premieres of this season were Edouard Lalo's *Roi d'Ys*, with Ponselle, Alda, Gigli, and Giuseppe Danise; Rimsky-Korsakov's *Snegurotchka,* with Bori—a lengthy Russian folk tale which in popularity never approached *Boris Godunov* or even the later *Sadko*; and Alfredo Catalani's *Loreley,* with Muzio, which had been planned as early as 1908. There were inconsistencies in these productions, especially of language. The Rimsky-Korsakov opera was given in French, like *Le Coq d'Or,* which came after it; Chaliapin sang Boris in Russian to his colleagues' Italian; and Jeritza sang *Lohengrin* in Moravian-accented German while the chorus carried on in English—though German had now been reinstated for *Tristan und Isolde* and the first *Walküre* since the war. President Harding had made peace with Germany and Austria. Prohibition had gone into effect; skyscrapers were reaching higher, and youth flamed.

The management's policy of building repertory around big stars had its hazards. With new singers of top caliber in short supply, one after another of the Company's earlier mainstays bowed out. On April 22, 1922, at the age of forty, Geraldine Farrar made her last appearance. The occasion might have been more auspicious than a matinee of Leoncavallo's *Zazà*: Farrar had in fact requested *Tosca* for her farewell, but Gatti, who had tried everything to make her stay on, was adamant about her singing the role originally scheduled as her last for the season. Following the matinee, the diva in an open touring car led a festive parade up Broadway, where amid a sea of bright banners and balloons excited crowds of "Gerryflappers" shouted farewell to their idol.

At the close of the 1921–1922 season—which had survived the loss of Caruso and Farrar, while adding four new stars, five new operas, and seven new productions—the Metropolitan directors showed their gratitude to Gatti by extending his contract

Farrar turns her back on the Metropolitan: As the heroine of Leoncavallo's *Zazà,* Geraldine Farrar (*opposite page*) caused her ultimate stir with this plunging dress. A month earlier, Frances Peralta and Florence Easton (*left*) portrayed the sisters Dorabella and Fiordiligi in the first U.S. performance of Mozart's *Così Fan Tutte,* March 24, 1922; that same year Lillian and Dorothy Gish (*below*) were seen as Orphans of the Storm in a silent film voted "best picture of the year."

through 1925–1926, though his current term still had a year to run. Knowing his box office, the shrewd general manager engaged another new star for 1922–1923: Elisabeth Rethberg, whose "high, clear, liquid tones of a singular brightness" floated over the orchestra at her debut as Aida. In the same production Sigrid Onegin was scarcely less imposing as Amneris. Lauri-Volpi also made his debut that season.

The following season "the high gods were restored" with Karin Branzell's arrival as Fricka; and a week later Friedrich Schorr brought an "unforced lyric beauty" to Wolfram in *Tannhäuser.* Both singers were to remain with the Metropolitan for many seasons, and in 1924–1925 they were joined by two other superb Wagnerians, Maria Müller and Nanny Larsen-Todsen. The twenty-three-year-old Czech soprano's Sieglinde was welcomed for its "grace and sincerity," while Larsen-Todsen made an equally good first impression less than a fortnight later as the Metropolitan's first postwar Brünnhilde (to Müller's Gutrune) in *Götterdämmerung.* The problem of finding a first-rate *Heldentenor* to match these artists was solved the next season, when Lauritz Melchior first stepped onto the Metropolitan scene. In his debut as Tannhäuser Melchior seemed uncomfortable, but his potential was instantly recognized, and he became the Company's leading Wagnerian tenor for twenty-four years.

Gatti's policy of alternating prima donnas on opening night proved so astute that he continued it for a decade. Onstage this policy helped camouflage the absence of Caruso, and in the pit Tullio Serafin—an importation of 1924—did much to restore the artistic impetus that had left the Italian wing with Toscanini. From the *Aida* of 1924–1925 through the *Peter Ibbetson* of 1933–1934, Serafin conducted every opening night, as well as many other operas from a diverse repertory; he even led a *Siegfried* (with his wife, Elena Rakowska, as Brünnhilde) and a *Parsifal.*

To Serafin's leadership Gatti early in 1925 entrusted the revival of *Falstaff.* Scotti sang the title role, but the chief honors went to a young baritone from California, Lawrence Tibbett (actually Tibbetts, but a typographical error in the program established him for posterity as Tibbett). Risen but recently from bit parts, he drew an ovation as Ford that recalled Campanari's debut in the role thirty years earlier. The following November the Italian conductor introduced Spontini's *Vestale* with a cast that rivaled the all-star *Huguenots* of the Grau regime: onstage were Ponselle, Matzenauer, De Luca, Mardones, and the new tenor Edward Johnson, who impressed Aldrich of the *Times* as "some-

thing more than a voice." Serafin also led Giordano's *Cena delle Beffe* (reviewed as "a dull and in no sense worthy" setting of Sem Benelli's play, known as *The Jest* when the Barrymores first presented it on Broadway), a double bill featuring Falla's *Vida Breve* and Stravinsky's *Rossignol* (with the composer in attendance), *Turandot,* the first Metropolitan *Norma* since Lilli Lehmann (with Ponselle now in the title role), and Deems Taylor's *King's Henchman.* The last was the first American opera produced at the House since the war, and interest in it centered as much on the libretto, by Edna St. Vincent Millay, as on Taylor's fluent, eclectic score. Unfortunately for intelligibility, however, Miss Millay had chosen to tell the *Tristan*-like story in words predating the Roman occupation of Britain.

If the Metropolitan's German and French repertory was not ignored during the twenties, in comparison with the revivals in Italian it can hardly be said to have flourished. Responsibility for this was not all the general manager's. Public interest did not rise, for instance, to the importance of Janáček's *Jenufa* (introduced for Jeritza in 1924–1925), and *Pelléas et Mélisande*—the Metropolitan's first, and New York's first since Mary Garden—proved a *succès d'estime,* though bouquets went to Bori and Johnson for their singing, to Wilhelm von Wymetal for his direction, and to Joseph Urban and his wife, Grete Thurlow, for the imaginative settings.

Despite censure of the Metropolitan's conservatism from some quarters (in 1922 Gatti-Casazza had dismissed Prokofiev after a piano trial of one act of his *Love for Three Oranges* with "Thank you, Maestro, that will be enough"), Gatti's contract was again renewed in 1925–1926, granting him tenure through 1930–1931. Kahn issued a statement praising the general manager as "characterized by steadfast adherence to high artistic standards," and some even suggested he should be appointed for life. To the inevitable criticism—that short-lived novelties had been depriving the standard repertory of attention, that Wagnerian productions were becoming increasingly shoddy—Gatti replied that he had been promised a new house (as indeed he had, as far back as 1908) and that when he got it he would see about doing the Teutons justice.

Gatti had recently added a second roof stage to facilitate rehearsals; other than this, the Metropolitan's technical facilities

A quartet of Gatti's stars: Giuseppe De Luca (*opposite page, left,* as Rigoletto) enhanced the Metropolitan's baritone wing from November 1915, Elisabeth Rethberg (shown as Maddalena in *Andrea Chénier*) the soprano wing from November 1922. Claudia Muzio (below her, as Aida) had just quit the soprano ranks after six seasons of stardom; baritone Antonio Scotti (*left*), in the middle of his remarkable tenure of thirty-four seasons, had long relished a role tailor-made for him, Chim-Fen in *L'Oracolo*.

had seen no improvement in about a dozen years. The new addition filled out the southwestern quarter of the house and balanced the lopsided Seventh Avenue silhouette. No further alterations were to be made for more than a decade, chiefly because Kahn kept thinking that the new opera house he dreamed of was about to materialize.

Several uptown sites that were being considered eventually narrowed down to one, at Fifty-seventh Street west of Eighth Avenue, and Urban, working with another designer, actually started to plan the theater. But the scheme lacked unified backing, both in principle and in capital, and in 1928 the plans were shelved. Later projects, variously focused on Washington Square, Columbus Circle, and Rockefeller Center, also fell through, and it was not until the fifties that plans for Lincoln Center took shape.

Physical inadequacies of the Opera House were to blame, as much as anything, for displays of temperament with which Gatti had often to cope. When new artists were engaged there were no facilities for training them to work together. The patient schooling in dramatic technique that was practiced in the theater at the time, for example by Max Reinhardt and the Moscow Art Theatre, was not emulated at the Opera House. Consequently there were often flare-ups among the performers, many of whom could only sing, not speak, the language of their fellow artists; and the complications arising from jealousy, hurt feelings, or chagrin over what some critic had said could be major. There was the notorious performance of *Tosca* during which Maria Jeritza and Beniamino Gigli, as the lovers, bit and kicked each other in full view of the audience; they were forever afterward kept apart. But despite this and many other such episodes, requiring all the manager's diplomacy and powers of persuasion to keep the performers safe from mayhem and able to appear before the footlights, Gatti's regime continued to show a profit.

In 1926 a ballyhoo and flurry of ticket speculation, unmatched since the world premiere of *La Fanciulla del West*, preceded the debut in *Rigoletto* of Marion Talley, a girl of eighteen from Kansas City. "A few years ago the house was not a kindergarten," snorted W. J. Henderson. "It is easier to achieve success in opera than it used to be," he added in a review that was certainly not calculated to give the teenager a firm start. Yet he quite failed to stop Miss Talley from attacking role after role for several years to come.

The 1926–1927 season had started with a most distinguished newcomer, Ezio Pinza, who sang *La Vestale* on opening night "with brains and discretion"—qualities that would see him enter musical comedy, late in his career, with equal aplomb. The following season brought Gertrude Kappel, whose Isolde was acknowledged the finest since Gadski's, before the war. And then, on February 7, 1928, a girl from Tennessee, whose successes at the Metropolitan were far to exceed those of Miss Talley, made her debut as Mimi. Grace Moore drew only tentative musical approbation, but Francis D. Perkins in the *Tribune* noted that the former singer from Broadway's *Music Box Revue* seemed "at home on the stage." And so she remained—at home equally in films and on radio—until her death in a plane crash nearly two decades later.

A mixture of disillusion and bullish euphoria infected the Opera House at the opening of its 1928–1929 season; hopes of a new Metropolitan had by then been dashed, but in the old Metropolitan, opera seemed to be getting better and better. The management did not need the late, fashionable Dr. Emile Coué to tell it so: it had only to look at its own roster and repertory with one eye and at its ledger books with the other.

Audiences saw some stylish new presentations that winter: four American premieres, two important revivals, and several noteworthy ensembles. On opening night, October 29, *L'Amore dei Tre Re* united Ponselle, Martinelli, Danise, and Pinza under the baton of Serafin. The same singers, but with Titta Ruffo in place of Danise, figured in *Ernani*—the last performance of the work to be heard at the Metropolitan for twenty-seven seasons. Melchior sang his first local *Tristan* and *Götterdämmerung* and on April 1, 1929, *Der Freischütz* bowed out of the repertory for good.

The four new operas were contemporary. This impressive accomplishment, though not without precedent, has never since been duplicated. Joseph Urban undertook to design all four productions, and went to work creating sets and costumes that ranged in period from legendary antiquity to the present. *Die Aegyptische Helena*, a fanciful postscript to the Trojan War by Richard Strauss and Hugo von Hofmannsthal, was notable for the presence of Maria Jeritza in the title role; but W. J. Henderson complained that "The Metropolitan has known [no libretto] more puerile, more futile or less interesting. . . . Strauss has furnished . . . nothing new." The press was equally indifferent toward *Fra Gherardo*, a somber tale of thirteenth-century Parma by Ildebrando Pizzetti, and toward Ottorino Respighi's *Campana Sommersa*, with a stellar cast of Rethberg, Martinelli, De Luca, and Pinza, though both composers were present and took repeated bows.

Meanwhile, on more progressive stages: Konstantin Stanislavski and his Moscow Art Theatre were giving this look—unified staging, "interpretive" costuming—to *Carmencita and the Soldier* (*below*), a version of Mérimée's tale. But the stage picture on Broadway and Thirty-ninth Street adhered to a safe, conservative path; witness Maria Jeritza (*left, with Albert Einstein*) in her *Carmen* Act IV costume.

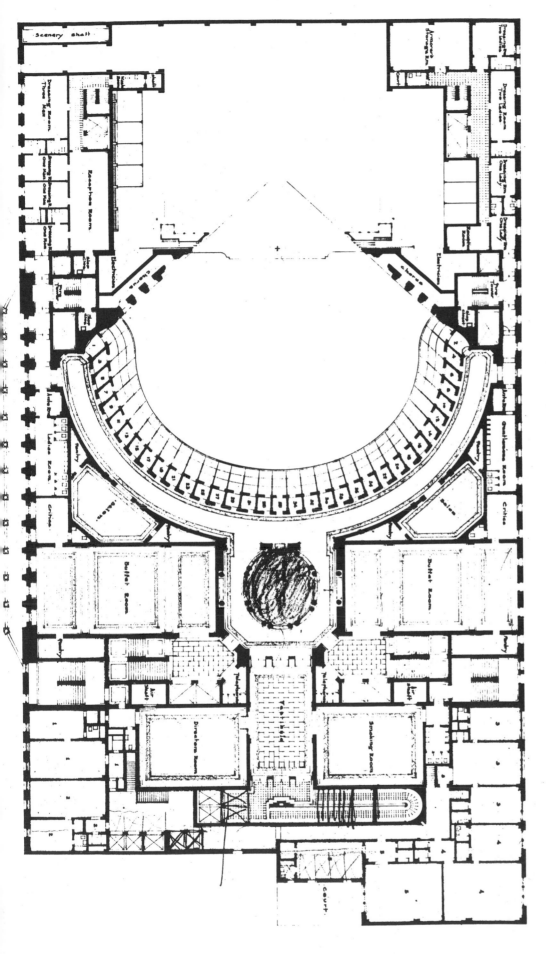

The dream of a new Opera House: With the encouragement of Otto Kahn, Joseph Urban worked up plans for a vastly improved physical plant on a West Fifty-seventh Street plot Kahn had secured (1927). It fell through, though many of its features—the proscenium, the extended stage apron, the broad rather than deep fan shape, resulting in flawless sight lines —were incorporated in Radio City Music Hall (1932).

Highlights of the roaring twenties: Rosa Ponselle received an ovation for her Giulia in the first Metropolitan *La Vestale* and the *Norma* that followed. In both cases the conductor was Tullio Serafin (shown opposite on shipboard with Ponselle), the Italian who led four American operas in their world premieres at the Metropolitan between 1927 and 1934. One of them featured the trio seen below: Edward Johnson as tenor, Deems Taylor as composer, and Edna St. Vincent Millay as his librettist collaborated on *The King's Henchman.* Another ovation winner, Charles A. Lindbergh, rode up Broadway (*left,* with New York's Mayor Jimmy Walker) after his transatlantic solo flight, May 21, 1927.

What did get a rise out of the critics, as well as the audiences, was the fourth new opera: a jazz satire, *Jonny Spielt Auf,* by Ernst Křenek. The Viennese composer's protagonist, a Negro saxophonist (performed in blackface by Michael Bohnen and Lawrence Tibbett), played seven performances in the august confines of the Opera House and ended each one symbolically astride the world. Though sung in German, the work stirred comparisons with Gilbert and Sullivan, as well as "general excitement and discussion . . . deep satisfaction." Much was being said in those days of the "marriage" of jazz and serious music, sanctioned by such high priests as Paul Whiteman and George Gershwin. "The foxtrotting of Křenek is pretty heavy business," noted Henderson in his review in the *Sun,* but he added, "This is pretty good musical comedy."

It appeared that the Metropolitan, at forty-five, was cutting up before permanently settling down. The jazz mania, however, went deeper than appearances: it summed up an attitude toward life and license. "Everything that appeals to our generation," wrote another observer, "finds its place in *Jonny*—the film, broadcasting, loudspeaker, exoticism, revues, luxurious hotels and motorcars and express trains." The first talking picture, *The Jazz Singer,* had been shown in New York in 1927. Two months before the opening of the 1928–1929 season, a more vitriolic and hence more viable satire, Kurt Weill's *Dreigroschenoper,* had caused a storm in Berlin; two weeks before the Metropolitan opened, the dirigible *Graf Zeppelin* had arrived from Germany with twenty passengers and a crew of thirty-eight. It was hard to tell which was accelerating faster, lavish living or the mockery of it.

Accelerating wealth made it all possible. The price of Opera House tickets, with an $8.25 top, was the highest it had ever been and higher than it would be again until 1954–1955. The Metropolitan's income during this boom season of 1928–1929 was the highest in its history: $3,111,805, with a net profit of $90,937 after expenses. Thanks to the acumen of the general manager, the Company had $2,000,000 in the bank, and as the Metropolitan prepared to open its next season, on October 28, 1929, checks were already in hand for subscription renewals. Events would soon prove that this was a fortunate if unintentional stroke of foresight.

While Titta Ruffo (*opposite page, right,* as Cascart in *Zazà*) was holding his own in the Italian wing, Lauritz Melchior and Marion Talley made their debuts—he as Tannhäuser, she as Philine in *Mignon.*

Farewell to an age: Three Metropolitan stars—
Frances Alda, Amelita Galli-Curci, Margarete
Matzenauer—sang their last during the
1929–1930 season. The final appearance of
Alda, who was no longer Mrs. Gatti-Casazza,
took place as Puccini's Manon Lescaut on
December 28; she is shown here with Gigli
(who had sung her Chevalier Des Grieux)
and, left to right, Edward Johnson, Giulio Setti,
Antonio Scotti, Lucrezia Bori (a rival in
the role), Pavel Ludikar, Lawrence Tibbett,
Giovanni Martino, and Giovanni Martinelli.

Betwixt Prohibition and Repeal: Congress
passed the Eighteenth Amendment in 1919,
the Twenty-first Amendment in 1933; in
between came the (legally) dry period and
rituals characteristic of the twenties—the
basement speakeasy, for instance, or Grace
Moore playing Giulietta in *Les Contes
d'Hoffmann* (to Tibbett's Dappertutto,
opposite). None was more sumptuously staged
than the symbolic marriage at the end of
Puccini's *Turandot*. Left are Giacomo
Lauri-Volpi and Maria Jeritza in the American
premiere, heard at the Metropolitan in
1926–1927.

Jazz doth bestride the narrow world: The grand finale of Křenek's *Jonny Spielt Auf,* with Lawrence Tibbett in blackface and Joseph Urban's settings (*opposite*), set Opera House audiences of 1929 on their ear. Though the dirigible *Graf Zeppelin,* passing close by the Metropolitan, may have suggested that everything in 1929 was indeed airborne, *Variety*'s famous headline (*above*) on the stock-market crash had the sobering effect of the morning after.

The End of an Era
1929–1935

As the audience began to fill the Golden Horseshoe on October 28, 1929, for the opening night that was to inaugurate the new season—the best season, some said, that the Metropolitan had ever looked forward to—who among the glittering first-nighters could have foreseen the events of the next day? Otto Kahn, perhaps. Before nightfall of October 29, sixteen million shares had changed hands on the New York Stock Exchange. By an ironical coincidence, the opera that opened the season was *Manon Lescaut,* in which the heroine goes broke. The great Wall Street bubble had finally burst, and fortunes evaporated overnight.

Kahn's own fortune may have remained intact, but his days as Maecenas were nearly over. In 1931, suffering from the beginnings of tuberculosis, he resigned from the board of directors. His position was taken by Paul D. Cravath, under whose aegis the new Metropolitan Opera Association, Inc., was formed in time for the 1932–1933 season.

In the very depths of the Depression, the courage, foresight, resourcefulness, and dedication of the management, performers, and certain key subscribers made it possible for opera to continue. The backlog of funds the Metropolitan had accumulated over its recent record-breaking years helped save the day in 1930–1931 when subscribers no longer affluent began to defect. But the reserves were not nearly enough, and as cancellations reached a danger point the stars helped the management to drum up business. Lucrezia Bori invited erstwhile subscribers to tea and persuaded many to renew; in 1932–1933 she joined Edward Johnson, Lawrence Tibbett, and Geraldine Farrar (who came out of retirement for the occasion) in a plea to the radio audience for funds. Miraculously the goal of $300,000 was reached, after a month of intensive campaigning aided by a series of benefit performances at the Opera House.

Meanwhile radio had penetrated the august defenses of the Metropolitan. Following a historic Christmas broadcast of *Hänsel und Gretel* in 1931, a series of hour-long samplings of Saturday matinee performances went on the air from coast to coast. At first Gatti-Casazza had been suspicious of the quality of musical sound that radio could provide, but after a private demonstration in his office he was persuaded to allow the broadcasts. The prospect of subsidy from a sponsor (at first, the NBC network itself) and of the Metropolitan Opera's reaching a large untapped public was too promising to resist. At first the technicians had to bring in their cumbersome equipment for each broadcast, while Deems Taylor, the intermission commentator, and Milton Cross, the announcer—as he has been throughout the entire series of programs from the Opera House—huddled in the antechamber of Box 44 on the Grand Tier. Members of the audience may have resented having to pick their way over cables or being robbed of their exclusive prerogative of hearing opera; but the coming of radio enhanced the prestige of the Metropolitan.

In repertory, too, Gatti-Casazza kept the old abreast of the new. The 1929–1930 season had seen a revival of *La Fanciulla del West,* the first since 1913–1914; Verdi's *Luisa Miller* was new to the Opera House, displaying the talents of Ponselle as *Norma* had done; and *Don Giovanni* performed a similar service for Ezio Pinza, who helped to make the work a success after it had been absent from the repertory for two decades. The general manager's trump card that season was the "sumptuous spectacle" designed by Serge Soudeikine for Rimsky-Korsakov's *Sadko.* In this the music made less of an impression than the ballet, with choreography by Rosina Galli and August Berger.

Further notes of escapism were sounded in 1930–1931: gaiety in Franz von Suppé's frothy *Boccaccio* for Jeritza, nostalgia in Deems Taylor's *Peter Ibbetson,* with its dream view of life. The glow of Jaromir Weinberger's Czech folk opera *Schwanda,* "overflowing with catchy music," was offset in the 1931–1932 season by the dullness of Montemezzi's "wholly undistinguished" *Notte di Zoraima* and the somber tone of Verdi's *Simon Boccanegra*—new to the Metropolitan and surprisingly a hit. This was owing to the popularity of Lawrence Tibbett, whose training as an actor enabled him to bring more to the principal role than a voice.

Despite the well-balanced fare, subscriptions fell off drastically, and the management decided to cut ticket prices the next season and reduce the number of performances. Financial pressures of the Depression saved Gatti only one worry: what to do about the salary spiral. Back in March 1929 he had had to pay Chaliapin $3,500 for a single *Boris Godunov* in Philadelphia; and many singers had begun to bypass the Metropolitan in favor of the Chicago Opera, where Samuel Insull, bent on proving his opera company second to none, was offering astronomical fees to lure talent away from New York. After the crash, with Insull forced to retrench, the Metropolitan was relieved of a threat even greater than Hammerstein. Gatti himself offered to work for nothing if necessary, and when he asked members of the Company to take 10-per-cent salary cuts he lost only one star, Gigli.

The first world premiere to be broadcast from the Metropolitan stage—on January 7, 1933—brought *The Emperor Jones* to an audience of millions, who unfortunately could not see Tibbett's title role (*opposite*).

The jungle comes to the Metropolitan: A new kind of musical theater burst upon the scene with Louis Gruenberg's *Emperor Jones.* Eugene O'Neill had furnished the story, Tullio Serafin conducted, Jo Mielziner designed the production.

Two kinds of Americana: Though Montemezzi's *Notte di Zoraima* (*opposite page,* with Rosa Ponselle in the title role and Mario Basiola as Pedrito) dealt with a revolt among the Incas of Peru, it failed to last more than four North American performances in 1931–1932. Somewhat more staying power was displayed by Ann Lawanick and Jack Ritof, who are shown as they approached the 1,145-hour mark of a dance marathon staged at the Merry Garden Ballroom in Chicago.

LUNCHEONETTE SERVICE
RINGSIDE
OR IN THE FOUNTAIN ROOM

The first Metropolitan broadcast, *Hänsel und Gretel* with Editha Fleischer and Queena Mario (*opposite page*), on Christmas Day, 1931, introduced opera to a vast new audience when the Opera House exchequer needed it most. But announcer Milton Cross (*left,* rear) worked against great odds in Box 44.

In 1932, the year voters pinned their hopes on a New Deal, the Metropolitan roster gained some important new stars. Gladys Swarthout and Lily Pons had recently joined the Company, and now two prima donnas, Frida Leider and Maria Olszewska, both formerly with the Chicago Opera, made their local debuts in *Tristan und Isolde.* There were other debuts—Tito Schipa, Rose Bampton, Richard Bonelli, Richard Crooks—and the farewell of Caruso's friend Antonio Scotti. The baritone ended thirty-three seasons with the Metropolitan in a performance of *L'Oracolo,* a tale of San Francisco's Chinatown composed for him by Franco Leoni. Strauss's *Elektra,* unheard in New York since Hammerstein's production at the Manhattan Opera House twenty-three years before, was added to the repertory. And Tibbett made a great hit in the world premiere of Louis Gruenberg's *Emperor Jones,* based on the play by Eugene O'Neill.

These signs of vigor notwithstanding, the ensuing season, 1933–1934, was cut to fourteen weeks—the shortest yet in the history of the Company. It opened the day after Christmas (following a pre-season *Hänsel und Gretel*) with *Peter Ibbetson,* the first American opera to inaugurate a season at the Metropolitan. The Juilliard Foundation, which commissioned Deems Taylor to write the work, was also among those answering the Metropolitan's pleas for contributions. Another American work, Howard Hanson's *Merry Mount,* had its world premiere at a Saturday broadcast matinee with Tibbett singing the role of a preacher in Puritan New England wrestling with temptations of the flesh. *Salome* was given for the first time since 1907, the way for the revival having been paved by *Elektra.* The earlier Strauss shocker raised few eyebrows now; in fact, some observers judged the performance too sedate, though one critic found Göta Ljungberg's singing and dancing in the title role was "nearer Broadway than the River Jordan."

March 28, 1934, saw a performance of *Parsifal.* The next day Otto Kahn died in his New York office, and the second *Parsifal,* scheduled for March 30, was dedicated to his memory. His endowments and his flamboyance—like those of David Belasco, with whom he had kept in touch until the impresario's death in 1931—now belonged to Metropolitan history. Kahn had not been able to dislodge the directors from their boxhold in a building that epitomized the established order. They had been willing to have him pay the deficits but had not let him lead them uptown to a new opera house. Otherwise, Kahn's behind-the-scenes rule had been absolute. He had underwritten to the fullest Gatti's repertory experiments, even if few exhibited staying power. Both men

had encouraged American singers and developed a brilliant (and expensive) international roster of stars—Martinelli, Ponselle, Rethberg, Tibbett, Melchior, Pinza, Moore, Swarthout, Pons, Crooks, Lotte Lehmann. Kahn's last great acquisition—though he did not live to hear her debut—was Flagstad. Through Gatti, Kahn had established the Metropolitan rule that an opera should be performed in its original language whenever possible. Having anticipated and barely outlived the optimistic mood of the 1920's, Kahn had helped make possible its characteristic achievements: a record length of season (twenty-four weeks from 1923 to 1932), a record number of performances per season (194 in 1925–1926), a record number of works per season (forty-nine in 1927–1928). And Kahn had also encouraged the start of regular broadcasting.

Having laid its guardian angel to rest, the Metropolitan faced the last season of another familiar figure, its general manager. When Gatti-Casazza, tired and no longer either young or well, announced that the 1934–1935 season would be his last, he signaled the end of an era. For more than two decades Gatti had presided over an artistic empire unparalleled for stability and prosperity. But its taste showed signs of growing effete; its oligarchy, heirs of the original boxholders, had lost much of their will and means to rule; its emphasis on smooth-running organization, rather than on the often erratic pursuit of excellence, had made it somewhat ponderous.

Who knows whether the story would have been different if the Metropolitan had moved to the better physical plant uptown that Kahn and Gatti dreamed of? Air-conditioning, improved sight lines, adequate storage space would have to wait for a new house; meanwhile the Metropolitan could and did make some improvements in the old: circulating ice water, more comfortable Orchestra seats, new terrazzo floors in the lobbies, and more comfortable upholstered seats in the Family Circle. The Fire Department decreed a new asbestos fire curtain. And there were changes in electrical wiring and equipment, including a new stage switchboard, which made better lighting effects possible.

The improvements were external as well: in preparation for the 1934–1935 season the Opera House had three of its façades cleaned by sandblasting. Only the rear, facing Seventh Avenue, was ignored—perhaps on the theory that it was an architectural

Kirsten Flagstad, shown opposite as Kundry in *Parsifal,* a role she learned in eleven days, was bestowed by Gatti upon his successor, Edward Johnson, as Caruso had been passed along to Gatti by Conried.

Staging Wagner during the thirties: While the Rhinemaidens (*opposite page*) were discovering the perils of travel in a sort of breeches buoy, the Knights of the Grail were sitting in business suits watching Amfortas rehearse under the eagle eyes of coach Pietro Cimara and stage director Wilhelm von Wymetal.

"A very affecting drama with slow music": This was Olin Downes' appraisal of *Peter Ibbetson,* the Deems Taylor opera, which clung to a way of life that was fading even as Bori (Duchess of Towers, left) and Johnson (in the title role, beside her) created it on the stage of the Opera House.

jumble anyway, made more of an eyesore by scenery stacked against its walls. This face-lifting, long overdue, seemed a brave attempt to deny the harsh truth: at fifty-one the *grand dame* of United States musical institutions had passed her prime.

The opera season itself was hale enough, however. It included an opening-night *Aida* with Rethberg, Martinelli, and Tibbett, and a successful premiere of Pergolesi's *Serva Padrona,* broadcast on the afternoon of February 23. The *Ring* cycle returned, as did *Der Rosenkavalier* (with Lehmann, Olszewska, List). *Don Pasquale,* absent for thirty seasons, was brilliantly performed by Bori, Schipa, De Luca, and Pinza in a production by the new designer Jonel Jorgulesco. And on February 2 there was the unheralded debut, in a broadcast matinee of *Die Walküre,* of Kirsten Flagstad, a little-known soprano of thirty-nine whom Otto Kahn had heard in Scandinavia as early as 1929.

Flagstad's arrival could scarcely have been more timely. The ranking Wagnerian, Frida Leider, had decided not to return—on the grounds that the brevity of the Metropolitan season made the long steamship voyage from Germany hardly worth her while—and another Wagnerian soprano, Anny Konetzni, had met with little success in New York. Flagstad gave the languishing German repertory a shot in the arm; her initial Sieglinde caused a furor resulting in her appearance, in quick succession, in six other Wagnerian roles. "For once," wrote Olin Downes, "the Metropolitan has engaged a singer who is in her prime." And Flagstad had been on the point of retiring when Gatti engaged her!

Flagstad's conductor was the energetic Artur Bodanzky. He shared the podium that season with Vincenzo Bellezza, Wilfrid Pelletier, and Ettore Panizza, the last a worthy successor to Serafin. Two *Don Giovanni*s were given in 1934–1935. *Fidelio* had to be canceled. The last of Gatti's novelties, Laurence Seymour's *In the Pasha's Garden,* the vehicle for Helen Jepson's debut, proved no more successful than many of its predecessors, in spite of scenic projections by Frederick J. Kiesler—the first appearance of such a device on the Metropolitan stage.

If Gatti's valedictory season was hardly a crowning glory, he could look back on a remarkable achievement. Of some two hundred operas given in more than five thousand performances during his tenure, half were works he had introduced to the repertory. Twenty-five operas have been given world premieres at the Metropolitan, twenty-one of them in Gatti's reign; four were by Puccini, a dozen by United States composers. Of the eighty-two American premieres at the Opera House, fifty were under Gatti; these ranged from *Così Fan Tutte* and Gluck's *Iphigénie en Tau-*

ride to contemporary works heard within a year or two of their first performance, such as *Der Rosenkavalier, L'Amore dei Tre Re,* and *Turandot.* If the opera world no longer esteems the works of Gatti's countrymen Zandonai, Franchetti, Lattuada, Catalani, Riccitelli, Leoni, and Vittadini, it has also forgotten such non-Italians as Thuille, Blech, Leroux, Weiss, and Schillings, to whose works he extended a welcome equally out of keeping with their promise. Though a son of the Mediterranean, Gatti feared no invaders from the North or East: among the operas to which he gave first performances in America were *The Bartered Bride* and *Pique Dame; Le Coq d'Or, Snegurotchka,* and *The Fair at Sorotchintsk; Boris Godunov, Prince Igor,* and *Eugene Onegin.*

The decade after Gatti retired saw great changes in opera. Numbers of those who made (rather than inherited) money came to rent (rather than buy) boxes at the Metropolitan. And with the passage in 1935 of the Social Security Act and the founding in the same year of the Committee for Industrial Organization (C.I.O.), the musicians at the Opera became a social force; their orchestra too joined a union, while in 1936 the singers banded together as AGMA (American Guild of Musical Artists).

Even in the throes of the Depression, with its breadlines, apple venders, and scenes of misery in the streets, New York was being transformed. Landmarks under construction gave the city a new face—the George Washington Bridge, Empire State Building, and Radio City Music Hall.

When Gatti-Casazza bade this New World farewell, sailing on the *Rex* in April 1935, members of the Company tried to banish their sadness with a parade on the Lido Deck. Rosa Ponselle gave a party under a banner reading "Long Live Our Beloved Gatti," and everyone kissed him on both cheeks.

In May 1935, the month after Gatti's departure, the world's largest ship, the *Normandie,* arrived in New York on her maiden voyage. The French liner's lavish splendor was to be short-lived: only a few years later she burned and capsized at her pier. The old order was ending, and sandblasting could not gloss the fact for those concerned with the future of the Opera House. Otto Kahn, who predicted the Second World War, did not live to see it, and Giulio Gatti-Casazza saw only its beginning. But Hitler, whom Kahn recognized as anti-human, and Mussolini, whom he and Gatti innocently admired, were preparing to shift the scenes.

Gatti's Pax Romana ended, appropriately, on the Lido Deck of the *Rex,* where Rosa Ponselle (at his left) gave a party for the departing general manager and his second wife, Rosina Galli (with wreath).

The cold facts, the warm fancy: Though in 1930 the giant journalist Heywood Broun was lending a helping hand in the breadlines (*opposite, above*), a season later Lily Pons (*left*) was unveiling her Lakmé before audiences ready to forget hunger and misery. Wagnerian forms of otherworldliness were largely in the hands of the two men at the café table—bass Friedrich Schorr and conductor Artur Bodanzky.

Highlights of Gatti's last season: Lotte Lehmann (photographed by Edward Steichen, *opposite page*) sang her first Metropolitan Marschallin in *Der Rosenkavalier* on January 4, 1935, and drew raves—something that Karin Branzell had been drawing for a decade with her Ortrud in *Lohengrin* (*left*), which she first sang at the Opera House on February 8, 1924, two nights after her debut.

In the teeth of the Depression: There was evidence of creative energy onstage and in the street. The year 1935, which saw George Gershwin join Todd Duncan, Anne Brown, and the other members of the cast after the New York opening of his *Porgy and Bess* (*opposite, above*), also saw the team of Ginger Rogers and Fred Astaire at the height of their popularity (*below,* in their film *Top Hat*). The Empire State Building (*left*) had set a standard of architectural ambition that remains unsurpassed; the "streamlined" design of Chrysler's Airflow car now proved a decade ahead of its time.

Entr'acte: The Audience Dresses Up

In the 1880's—the earliest years of the Metropolitan—women wore handmade and hand-trimmed dresses that swept the ground, men suffered in the grip of starched collars and cuffs, and it was social suicide to appear out of doors without a hat—a bowler or, better still, a top hat. Formal dress was *de rigueur* for those who watched the opera from their boxes, but even those holding modest seats wanted to "look like ladies and gentlemen." To a degree the custom has endured; some members of the audience have continued to dress for the opera, and not just on Monday, the fashionable subscription night.

Formality has been encouraged through the years by special occasions, white-tie affairs when the audience enjoys outdoing itself. In addition to opening nights, these field days for the couturier have been extended to charity benefits. And from the start charity often began at home. From 1883 till 1908 a benefit program was the accepted way of augmenting the general manager's income or that of an especially renowned star.

To attract the public on such occasions an all-star cast was organized. A large audience in 1896 saw a benefit program for the Abbey-Grau management, presenting selections from *La Favorita* (with Plançon), *Carmen* (Calvé), *Falstaff* (Maurel), *Lucia di Lammermoor* (Melba), *Faust* (the Soldiers' Chorus sung by all the stars of the Company), *Aida* (Nordica, Kaschmann, De Reszke), and again *Faust* (the Prison Scene, with Melba and the De Reszke brothers). On February 16, 1905, they gathered to see a "Director's Benefit" for Heinrich Conried, a *Fledermaus* with Marcella Sembrich—interrupted in Act II for a concert by Eames, Fremstad, Nordica, Caruso, Journet, and Scotti, among others!

Festive programs were often given in honor of V.I.P.s, the proximity of royalty providing boxholders with the perfect excuse to don tiaras and jeweled shirt-studs. In 1902 the architect Stanford White broke all precedents when he decorated the auditorium for the gala for Prince Henry of Prussia, with the outline of the royal yacht picked out in electric lights on the Opera House roof. The take that evening was a substantial $60,000, even though the house was not filled. After a late curtain—many in the audience followed the royal example by arriving after nine—the evening wore on through a miscellaneous program by the reigning singers of the day. The festivities were somewhat derailed when Marcella Sembrich, learning of the royal party's departure

The first ball at the Metropolitan: Matthew Arnold was one of the guests on January 3, 1884, a benefit for the Nursery and Children's Hospital. The Orchestra floor was raised to stage level, a tent added.

182

Two princes and a queen: Visiting royalty has been honored by gala performances on at least three occasions—Prince Henry of Prussia on February 25, 1902 (silk program on opposite page); the then Prince of Wales on November 18, 1919; and Queen Frederika of Greece (*left,* with Grover Whalen), on December 2, 1953.

(together with most of the audience) at 12:20 A.M., refused to go on for what was to have been the penultimate "number." The evening concluded with a scene from *Le Cid,* bravely sung by Bréval and Alvarez to an almost empty house.

Another gala was given for the Prince of Wales (on November 18, 1919), and the glamorous young man, later to reign briefly as Edward VIII, was an entr'acte few wished to miss. Throughout the years reigning monarchs and other dignitaries have often graced the Metropolitan audience, their presence always lending a special air to the proceedings.

Potpourri programs were often given, and perhaps reached the height of their popularity in the thirties, with the "Surprise Parties" given annually from 1931 to 1935 to offset Depression deficits. At the fourth of these parties, on March 31, 1935, $14,-000 was raised for the Maintenance Fund with a program that ended with stars spoofing their sacred opera. Items included "Der Wurm Turns," a Wagnerian travesty by Lawrence Tibbett; movie-style previews of "Coming [Opera] Attractions"; Broadway star Vandy Cape parodying an amateur singer, in answer to the perennial demand for more "local talent"; a jazzed-up *Aida* ballet; and a marathon "Nibelung Ringling Brothers" abbreviation of the *Ring,* with sixteen singers performing simultaneously in four circus rings. Lily Pons and Lauritz Melchior came onstage in tights for an acrobatic act that so alarmed one lady in the audience that she fainted. Nothing daunted, the featherweight soprano came on again in "Minnie the Moocher," with Helen Jepson and Gladys Swarthout, to the raucous strains of Chick Webb's dance band. The high point of the evening, however, was Beatrice Lillie's interpretation of Act I of *Carmen.* The British comedienne sang the role in a pastiche of real and invented languages and bit a chorister on the leg. At the close of the program a collegiate *Pagliacci,* complete with bleachers and cheerleaders, dissolved at the line "La commedia è finita!" into a sentimental tribute to Gatti-Casazza, who was retiring that season. The general manager, who would not appear onstage, was impersonated by the bass Emanuel List wearing a rubber mask.

Metropolitan audiences have always welcomed the opportunity to honor a singer or a manager at such a milestone in his career. Admirers helped Giovanni Martinelli celebrate both the twenty-fifth and the fiftieth anniversaries of his Metropolitan debut. And when Maria Jeritza returned long after her retirement—to sing in Rudolf Bing's production of *Fledermaus,* on Washington's Birthday, 1951—the audience found her, in her sixties, as blond and magnetic as ever. The farewells of Jean de Reszke, Fremstad, Sembrich, Farrar, Bori, Ponselle, Lotte Lehmann, and Flagstad were also occasions for tears and prolonged ovation.

Not all celebrations to do with the Metropolitan and its stars have been public, however. When Caruso came to America, he was given a reception not at the Opera House but at the home of Heinrich Conried. Anton Seidl, the musical director of the German seasons, lived and entertained—but not officially—in a suite in the Opera House. Some of the stars, notably Caruso and Emmy Destinn, were known for their generosity toward the "little people" backstage and in the offices, sometimes giving parties for them at their hotels. Singers often gave parties for other members of the Company, but only two—Flagstad and Bidù Sayão—ever commandeered the Opera House itself to play hostess to the entire personnel. During the last few years at the old House, the Association entertained the Company at an annual beer-and-sausages party with dancing.

Another sort of private celebration has been held by the various clubs connected with the Metropolitan. Stanford White helped to found one of these, a men's group known as the Vaudeville Club, and designed rooms for it in the Opera House during the 1892–1893 season, when the Metropolitan stood idle after its fire. As if to recapture the gaiety of college days, members of the club put on light shows after theater hours in a suite off the Grand Tier. Victor Herbert and Reginald De Koven came, and Nahan Franko led the club musicians—until a police raid one evening in 1898 put a stop to these lighthearted occasions and the club disbanded. Another such group, of later vintage, was the Ten Nights Club, made up of music critics who covered the ten performances the Metropolitan once gave annually in Brooklyn. During the teens and twenties they gave ribald skits on the roof stage, to which they invited Caruso, Jeritza, and other artists.

A less flamboyant organization, the Metropolitan Opera Club, succeeded the Vaudevillains in their quarters off the Grand Tier and since 1899 has continued to operate, its phalanx of white-tied "penguins" gracing the Club Box on the left of that Tier every Monday. Because of limited facilities, membership in the club is held to 125, plus 90 associate and junior members. For some years the club has held an annual champagne supper and opera ball after a non-subscription performance, to raise money for the Metropolitan.

William J. Guard, universally known as "Billy," built the original Metropolitan Opera press department; from 1911 to his death in 1932, he had a hand in all fêtes.

Surprise! surprise! for charity: Four Surprise Parties at the Opera House during the early thirties featured unannounced cutting-up by Metropolitan artists, including an apache dance by Lily Pons and Lauritz Melchior (*opposite page*), Beatrice Lillie's version of *Carmen* (*left,* Act I with Frederick Jagel as Don José), and the team of Pons, Swarthout, and Jepson singing "Minnie the Moocher" with Chick Webb's band.

The first ball at the Metropolitan took place midway in its maiden season, on January 3, 1884. A benefit for the Nursery and Children's Hospital, it proved to be the great social event of the New York winter; Matthew Arnold was among the many distinguished guests. On January 27, 1887, the Old Guard (New York State Militia) gave a ball in the House, and it was hoped, in vain, that President Cleveland would attend. The George Washington Centennial Ball on April 29, 1889, more successfully produced President Harrison, and Vice President Levi P. Morton as well. "Hundreds of men and women crowded the draughty stage," and massed saber flourishes could not steal the spotlight from such speakers as General Sherman, Whittier, Lowell, and Holmes. Purely social was the New Year's Ball of January 2, 1890, presided over by Ward McAllister, arbiter of "The 400." This attracted 1,100 guests, including Mrs. William Astor, whom McAllister took in to a supper of terrapin, partridge, and grouse—eight hot dishes and eight cold. The lobbies and boxes, filled with greenery, reminded some observers of hothouses.

On April 28, 1933, some 3,000 un-Depressed opera-lovers converged on the Opera House for the most elaborate social event in Metropolitan history: a costume ball in a Second Empire setting. Among the celebrities taking part in tableaux were Mrs. August Belmont as the Empress Eugénie, the French painter and illustrator Boutet de Monvel as Napoleon III, Walter Damrosch as Liszt, Edward Johnson as Prosper Mérimée, Sembrich as the Comtesse de Montijo, Lucrezia Bori as Patti, Grace Moore as Christine Nilsson. Frieda Hempel, as Jenny Lind, sang. The splendid showing netted a much-needed $25,000. However, the repeat endeavor the following year was much less successful. The 1934 setting moved to the court of Louis XV, with Monvel as the monarch, Damrosch as Bach, and Mary Pickford as a Hungarian princess. Ernest Schelling furnished a musical score, and Bori and Rosa Ponselle sang. Though two thousand people paid ten dollars apiece for this taste of the *ancien régime,* the cost of the ball was so enormous that little profit was left for the opera. The venture was repeated once more, on May 2, 1935. The scene this time was a New Orleans plantation with a "Magnolia and Orange Blossoms" motif. But the fashion for costume balls seemed to be fading, and after 1935 fund-raising shifted to gala performances.

The greatest dress-up occasion of all, opening night, was always on a Monday—the first night of that subscription series—until Rudolf Bing entered the scene in 1950. The new general manager, recognizing the special nature of opening night as well as the possibilities it offered for fund-raising, turned it into a non-subscription event, eventually at more than triple the old prices; tickets were offered to all subscribers and then to the public at large. The success of this tactic yielded all-time record proceeds of $108,737 at the 1964 opening, *Lucia di Lammermoor* with Joan Sutherland.

Opening night at the Metropolitan has occasionally coincided with some auspicious public event, as in 1918, when the season began on Armistice Day, and the audience "returned definitely to the diamond standard." Perhaps the dressiest opening night in recent times, and the only one not to have a complete opera as its program, was the performance of miscellaneous operatic acts over closed-circuit television at the start of the 1954–1955 season. The television cameras were trained as much on the audience as on the opera, enabling the entire country to share in the festivities. Opening night had been televised in 1948, 1949, and 1950, but the documentary value of these attempts had not offset the inconvenience of carting TV equipment into the Metropolitan and subjecting the audience to its glare and clutter. After 1954 it was decided to suspend television coverage until the new Opera House at Lincoln Center was built with adequate facilities.

Sensation-seekers have long found opening night—whether televised or not—a suitable arena for publicity. The show-off era began in 1939 with one Richard Knight, who stood on his head outside the Thirty-ninth Street entrance for the benefit of tabloid camera. The return of white tie in 1945 as the correct peacetime dress exerted a quieting effect, as did the presence of Mrs. Harry Truman and her daughter Margaret, who came to the opening that year to hear the latter's teacher, Helen Traubel, sing Elsa in *Lohengrin.* But 1947 found Mrs. Frank C. Henderson exposing an elderly leg on a table in Sherry's with the query, "What's Marlene got that I haven't got?" The end of such flamboyance came in 1949, with Mrs. Cornelius Vanderbilt's last appearance—brandishing a cane at photographers from her wheelchair—the season before Rudolf Bing took over as general manager.

The decline of high jinks with the rise of Bing was no mere coincidence. The new general manager soon proved himself a man who would sacrifice anything—even money—before dignity. If he remains unaware that the House, in its most depraved moment, once harbored a professional boxing match, it would be a kindness never to tell him.

Mrs. August Belmont (*opposite page*) came as the Empress Eugénie to the first Opera Ball, held on April 28, 1933; it netted $25,000 for the Metropolitan's favorite charity—the one that begins at home.

1789 — 1889

Centennial Celebration of the Inauguration, of George Washington, first President of the United States

DIAGRAM OF BOXES AND TABLES
FOR THE BANQUET OF THE
METROPOLITAN OPERA HOUSE
APRIL 30TH
1889.

DESIGNED AND ARRANGED BY
JOSEPH H. TAFT, Architect
146 Broadway
N.Y. City

PASSAGE

7TH AVENUE

PRESIDENTIAL TABLE.

PARTERRE ROW

FIRST TIER

Broadway.

ALL ODD NUMBERS OF SEATS AND BOXES ON 39TH ST. SIDE.

ALL EVEN NUMBERS OF SEATS AND BOXES ON 40TH ST. SIDE.

SOUTH SIDE BOXES ON 39TH STREET.

PARTERRE BOXES.

1. THOMAS HITCHCOCK,
3. R. T. WILSON,
5. JAMES A. BURDEN,
7. GEO. L. AND AMBROSE C. KINGSLAND,
9. WILLIAM ASTOR,
11. OGDEN GOELET,
13. HENRY I. BARBEY,
15. H. A. C. TAYLOR,
17. WILLIAM D. SLOANE,
19. WILLIAM G. HAMILTON,
21. VICTOR NEWCOMB,
23. CHAUNCEY M. DEPEW,
25. ELBRIDGE T. GERRY,
27. C. C. BALDWIN,
29. STUYVESANT FISH,
31. ROBERT C. WINTHROP,
33. ABRAM S. HEWITT,
35. HAMILTON FISH.

FIRST TIER BOXES.

37. S. B. ELKINS,
39. RESERVED BY OPERA HOUSE CO.,
41. MRS. MARSHALL O. ROBERTS,
43. G. G. HAVEN,
45. JAS. A. HAMILTON,
47. GEO. S. BOWDOIN,
49. EGERTON L. WINTHROP,
51. FREDERICK SHELDON,
53. EDWARD H. HARRIMAN,
55. S. L. M. BARLOW,
57. S. V. R. CRUGER,
59. MRS. PARAN STEVENS,
61. A. B. GARDINER,
63. HUGH J. GRANT,
65. SAMUEL D. BABCOCK,
67. MRS. N. BAYLIES,
69. H. H. ANDERSON,
71. THEO. W. MYERS,
73. W. E. D. STOKES.

NORTH SIDE BOXES ON 40TH STREET.

PARTERRE BOXES.

2. CLARENCE A. SEWARD,
4. J. HAMPDEN ROBB,
6. C. O. ISELIN, JR.,
8. JAMES M. VARNUM,
10. BYAM K. STEVENS,
12. WARD McALLISTER,
14. HENRY CLEWS,
16. JAMES H. BERKMAN,
18. WILLIAM JAY,
20. ROBERT GOELET,
22. W. BAYARD CUTTING,
24. WILLIAM W. ASTOR,
26. LUTHER KOUNTZE,
28. JAMES P. KERNOCHAN,
30. SAMUEL F. BARGER,
32. W. SEWARD WEBB,
34. ADRIAN ISELIN,
36. L. P. MORTON.

FIRST TIER BOXES.

38. JOHN KEAN,
40. FREDERIC J. DePEYSTER,
42. W. C. SCHERMERHORN,
44. ELLIOTT and THEODORE ROOSEVELT,
46. GEORGE L. SCHUYLER,
48. J. P. MORGAN,
50. ROBERT L. CUTTING,
52. SETH B. FRENCH,
54. FREDERICK S. TALLMADGE,
56. CORNELIUS N. BLISS,
58. BRAYTON IVES,
60. HENRY G. MARQUAND,
62. HORATIO B. POTTER,
64. JOHN A. KING,
66. GEORGE BARCLAY WARD,
68. SMITH CLIFT,
70. CLARENCE W. BOWEN,
72. ALEXANDER BROWN.

STAGE BOXES.

A THE CHAIRMAN,
B GENERAL FITZGERALD,
C GENERAL SHERMAN,
D MRS. McELROY,
E MRS. GRANT,
F HON. R. B. HAYES,
G HON. GROVER CLEVELAND,
H HON. THOMAS F. BAYARD,
I EX-GOVERNORS OF NEW YORK,

THE PRESIDENT,
R THE MAYOR,
S THE GOVERNOR,
T THE VICE-PRESIDENT,
J HON. SAMUEL BORROWE,
K HON. JOHN H. V. ARNOLD,
L THE SECRETARY,
M THE LIEUTENANT GOVERNOR,
N ADMIRAL PORTER,

O THE COMMITTEE OF THE HOUSE OF REPRESENTATIVES,
P THE CHIEF JUDGE OF THE COURT OF APPEALS,
Q THE CHIEF JUSTICE OF THE U. S.,
U THE MEMBERS OF THE CABINET,
V THE COMMITTEE of the U. S. SENATE,
W GENERAL SCHOFIELD,
X GOVERNORS of STATES other than N.Y.

The Opera House in other guises: In addition to a ballroom, the Metropolitan has been transformed into a fair, a banquet hall, and a royal court. The Centennial Banquet of April 30, 1889 attracted not only "The 400" (and then some) but the President and Vice-President of the United States, the Chief Justice, a victorious Civil War general, and a couple of major poets. Some years later, the Astors' Fair (*below*) turned the auditorium into a street of shops for charity.

The musicians themselves dress up: A farewell dinner for Marcella Sembrich at the Hotel Astor, February 7, 1909, attracted many notables, among whom the sharp eye will pick out (beginning in left field) Andreas Dippel, Jan Paderewski beside his countrywoman, Walter Damrosch, Antonio Scotti, Enrico Caruso, Victor Herbert, and Louise Homer.

The World of Tomorrow
1935–1950

The new general manager of the Metropolitan, who took over at the beginning of the 1935–1936 season, was a Canadian of cosmopolitan background; as late as 1930 he had given his home address as Florence, Italy, and he had sung five seasons at La Scala under the name of Edoardo di Giovanni.

Plain Edward Johnson he had been born, in Guelph, Ontario, in 1881. He had gone to Italy to study voice and there married the daughter of a Portuguese viscount. At La Scala his roles included the first *Parsifal* heard in Italy. He sang with the Chicago Opera before making his debut at the Metropolitan in 1922, the year he was naturalized as an American citizen. By any measure Johnson's singing career, begun in a church choir, had been a success, especially for a non-European tenor. To his new post he brought personal charm and optimism, in addition to an understanding of performers' psychology and the problems of casting and rehearsal schedules.

Johnson was not the only singer to turn manager; Andreas Dippel too had been a tenor, and Herbert Witherspoon, who in the spring of 1935 was named to succeed Gatti-Casazza as general manager, was a bass. Johnson had been appointed at that time to assist Witherspoon with a single task: the organization and direction of a supplemental season of popular-priced opera, to be performed by young Americans. When Witherspoon died of a heart attack, on May 10, 1935, Johnson stepped into the larger job. Neither a businessman nor an administrator, Johnson had to rely on two invaluable associates: Edward Ziegler, a former newspaper critic who had been assistant general manager since 1916, and Earle R. Lewis, who had worked his way up from ticket-seller to box-office treasurer.

In their first season this team introduced singers of the magnitude of Dusolina Giannini, Bruna Castagna, René Maison, Anna Kaskas, and Charles Kullman, and the three great classics they chose to present on the first three nights that winter—*La Traviata, Die Walküre,* and *Faust*—were an impressive salute to the international repertory and cast. But many were disappointed that Witherspoon's plans for an entire post-season of operas by Americans, using Deems Taylor's two works (Johnson himself had sung in *Peter Ibbetson*), Hanson's *Merry Mount,* and Gruenberg's *Emperor Jones* as a nucleus, were dropped. Although Johnson steered a conservative course, the season saw many distin-

guished productions: Flagstad's *Fidelio,* opposite Maison; a new production of *La Traviata*; a revival of *La Rondine* for Bori; and *The Bartered Bride* and *Gianni Schicchi* in English. Ponselle had reduced her weight "heroically" for a controversial portrayal of Carmen, which she repeated the following season—her last, though she was just forty.

Ballet and stage design both reached a new height in the 1936 spring season, when George Balanchine directed a double-cast production of *Orfeo ed Euridice* designed by Pavel Tchelitchew. The Gluck opera was the climax of the first season in which Balanchine's American Ballet served as the *corps* of the Opera House; it was to remain Johnson's boldest step as general manager. The Balanchine-Tchelitchew *Orfeo,* proving overimaginative for Metropolitan subscribers, was superseded in two years by the more "classical" production that has pleased audiences off and on ever since. Nor were the other Balanchine productions, in the two following seasons he served as ballet master and choreographer—*Aida, Carmen,* a triple bill of Stravinsky ballets conducted by the composer—pleasing to the conservatives.

For all the new manager's efforts, he had to face the loss of several stars from the Gatti regime. Giuseppe De Luca dropped out (temporarily, it developed), and to everyone's sorrow both Lucrezia Bori and Florence Easton ended their long, versatile careers with the Company. On the credit side, however, some superlative new singers joined the Metropolitan during the next few seasons; among them were Bidù Sayão, Kerstin Thorborg, Zinka Milanov, Licia Albanese, Nicola Moscona, Jussi Bjoerling, Stella Roman, Jan Peerce, Kurt Baum, Astrid Varnay, Dorothy Kirsten, and James Melton.

One source of new talent was the radio contest, "Auditions of the Air," which started during Johnson's first season as manager. Commercial sponsorship of the program provided the Metropolitan with revenue that helped to make up for the fees it formerly levied on concert appearances by artists on the roster (a practice to which AGMA had now put a stop). During the fifteen years of Johnson's regime these auditions gained for the Company such notable singers as Eleanor Steber, Maxine Stellman, Leonard Warren, Mack Harrell, Margaret Harshaw, Patrice Munsel, Regina Resnik, Robert Merrill, and Frank Guarrera. Traditional means of seeking out talent were also continued, through private auditions and scouting—and other potential sources of revenue were explored and developed, such as the rental of shops on the Broadway side of the Opera House. Meanwhile the Auditions did much to publicize both the Metropolitan and its younger talent.

Edward Johnson's greatest gift to the Metropolitan as general manager was musical ensemble—the kind provided by Sayão and Pinza, for example, in *Le Nozze di Figaro,* which had languished for two decades.

The Metropolitan's most progressive staging: In the 1936 spring season George Balanchine produced a double-cast *Orfeo ed Euridice* that made use of Pavel Tchelitchew's décor (*opposite, above*) and costumes (*left*). Later his American Ballet, as *corps* of the Opera House for three seasons, also offered Stravinsky's *Jeu de Cartes* (*below*), conducted by the composer (*opposite, below,* in another kind of card game with Balanchine, Annabelle Lyon, and other dancers). It gave further evidence that such productions left the taste of opera subscribers far behind.

Indeed it was "to broaden the base of participation in support of grand opera" that Mrs. August Belmont, with an eye to the national audience, founded the Metropolitan Opera Guild in the year of Johnson's accession. The Guild at once began to underwrite improvements in the House. Incredible as it seems, the Metropolitan had no cyclorama for scenic projections until the Guild supplied one, in 1936. The following year, which also saw the installation of a new stage floor (10,325 square feet of pine), the Guild gave funds to improve the Musicians' Room and to assist in the redecoration of dressing rooms. While it did not supply the new gold curtain that was hung in 1940—a replica of the thirty-five-year-old original—the organization did salvage the old one, cutting it up into small mementoes which were sold for over $11,000 to aid the cause of student tickets.

In the late 1930's, plans were afoot to raise a much larger sum: the goal of $1,000,000 was set by a committee of 200 civic leaders, headed by George A. Sloan, to purchase the Opera House from its boxholders. When the goal was reached, and the sale accomplished, the company that owned the Opera House and set the policy became, for the first time, identical with the company that produced the operas. Half of the $1,300,000 raised was put aside for much-needed operating capital. Roughly one-third of the total came from the Guild, another from the subscribers, and the remaining third from the Metropolitan's radio audience, which in a decade had grown to influential proportions. Sponsorship of the Saturday afternoon broadcasts was assumed in the fall of 1940 by the Texas Company, and henceforth Milton Cross did his announcing from a glass-walled radio booth at the center of the Grand Tier.

If there were fears that the Diamond Horseshoe would promptly turn to paste, once the Opera House changed hands, they must have been allayed by the continuing presence of Mrs. Cornelius Vanderbilt in Box 3—and of an undeniable if new millionaire, Thomas J. Watson, in J. P. Morgan's old Box 35. More important to operagoers in general was the replacement of the Grand Tier boxes with nearly 300 excellent single seats, 60 of them earmarked for the Guild—which, 15,000 strong by 1940, also enjoyed its own lounge, formerly reserved for the press. More comfortable Balcony seats were installed, and the backstage plumbing was renovated.

While the Metropolitan was having its face lifted—not for the first time, nor the last—old Europe was having its map remade. These were the days of Munich and the Austrian *Anschluss,* and whatever the influx of opera-minded refugees from Hitler's Europe may have had to do with a return of prosperity to the Metropolitan box office, the number of European artists, many of them displaced, appearing on the stage and podium was impressive. In addition to such recently arrived singers as Jarmila Novotna and Alexander Kipnis, both of whom had sung in *Die Zauberflöte* in Salzburg under Toscanini in 1937, and who made their Metropolitan debuts in 1939–1940, there were those who had appeared regularly at the Metropolitan and were now unable to return to Europe. Among the latter were Lotte Lehmann, Emanuel List, Friedrich Schorr, and Herbert Janssen. At the same time Johnson developed a veritable *Who's Who* of the podium: Sir Thomas Beecham, Bruno Walter, George Szell, Fritz Busch. Beecham had achieved an admirable operatic record at Covent Garden, Szell at the Berlin State Opera until 1930, Walter at Salzburg and at the Vienna State Opera, Busch in the Mozart performances at the Glyndebourne Festival in the mid-1930's. Fritz Reiner and Fritz Stiedry later joined the conducting staff, and there were the unsung assistant conductors—some of whom had looked forward to major careers in Europe—who quite literally prepared the performances. To the orchestra pit at the Metropolitan came such men as the bassoonist Hugo Burghauser, former president of the Vienna Philharmonic.

Five weeks before the 1940–1941 season opened, the world-cruise liner *Empress of Britain* was torpedoed and sunk off Ireland. A few days before that, the New York World's Fair (to which the Metropolitan contributed nine Wagner performances) had terminated its second and final season. "The World of Tomorrow" had evaporated, along with the leisurely yesterdays. France had fallen before the German onslaught, and the Battle of Britain was on, by the time the new gold curtain rose on another opening-night performance at the Metropolitan.

The 1940–1941 season was the first and only one in which all six of the composers named on the proscenium of the Metropolitan were also represented on its stage. Operas by Beethoven and Gluck had never before been given in the same season: *Fidelio* was conducted by Bruno Walter, making his Metropolitan debut, and *Alceste* received its first performance in the House. The opening-night opera, *Un Ballo in Maschera,* had not been heard for a quarter of a century.

A cast that deserved to be repeated opened the 1939–1940 season in *Simon Boccanegra,* including not only Tibbett as the Doge of Genoa but his eventual successor, Leonard Warren, as Simon's enemy.

...OLITAN OPERA ASSOCIATION, INC.
MONDAY EVENING, NOV. 27th AT 8:15 O'CLOCK
OPENING PERFORMANCE
GIUSEPPE VERDI'S OPERA
SIMON BOCCANEGRA
(IN ITALIAN)
Mme. Rethberg
Messrs. Martinelli, Tibbett,
Pinza, Warren
Conductor, Mr. Panizza
BOX OFFICE OPEN
WEEK DAYS (EXCEPT TUESDAYS) 9 A.M. to 9 P.M.
TUESDAYS 9 A.M. to 5 P.M.
SUNDAYS 12 NOON to 9 P.M.

Brave new world: Though Hitler was shortly to march into Poland, the New York World's Fair put on a show of optimistic progress in the summer of 1939 (*left*, Trylon and Perisphere). The following summer, progress reached the Opera House: the Grand Tier boxes gave way to 300 individual seats. The continuous democratic curve is shown on the opposite page in the process of construction and (*below*) during intermission of one of the Student Performances the new Metropolitan Opera Guild had started sponsoring in 1937.

The season saw the debuts of two notable singers, both of which took place on December 7, 1940, just a year before the bombing of Pearl Harbor. Radio listeners from coast to coast first heard Salvatore Baccaloni as Doctor Bartolo in the matinee of *Le Nozze di Figaro,* which had returned to the repertory the previous February after an absence of twenty-two seasons. (It was the first broadcast sponsored by the Texas Company.) Eleanor Steber sang her first Metropolitan performance as Sophie in the evening's *Rosenkavalier.* The war in Europe forced the cancellation of Germaine Lubin's debut as Alcestis, and Marjorie Lawrence, the Australian soprano who had made her debut in Edward Johnson's first season, took over the role in the Gluck opera. Five months later Miss Lawrence fell victim to polio in Mexico City.

The same pair of performances, on December 7, featured other stars whose names were to endure at the Metropolitan: Albanese, Novotna, Brownlee, and De Paolis in *Figaro,* Stevens, Votipka, Kaskas, Darcy, Cordon, and conductor Erich Leinsdorf in *Rosenkavalier.* Risë Stevens, a New York mezzo-soprano blessed with glamor of both voice and person, had set an example for an entire generation of American singers by declining a Metropolitan contract until she had had a chance to gain stage experience abroad (and to be coached by Richard Strauss). Because of the war, however, few young artists could follow this course.

Box-office income from the 1940–1941 season was $1,860,-511, the highest since 1930–1931. One reason may have been the public's interest in three beautifully designed new productions. The opening-night *Ballo in Maschera* introduced the designer Mstislav Dobujinsky: *Alceste* had sets and costumes by Richard Rychtarik; and for the new *Trovatore* Harry Horner won as much acclaim as for his *Orfeo ed Euridice,* first seen on November 26, 1938. Perhaps it was due to the freshness of these artists that the Metropolitan began to credit designers with specific productions.

But the main drawing card at the box office continued to be Kirsten Flagstad. The singer had surprised even the seasoned Bodanzky, one of those who had first auditioned her. To begin with, Flagstad had been engaged to fill secondary roles and as a replacement, but as soon as the management saw and heard her sing onstage everything changed overnight. (A similar reception was accorded Flagstad's successor, Helen Traubel, who did well in her debut—the world premiere of Walter Damrosch's *Man Without a Country* during the 1936–1937 season—but was not engaged again until 1939, and then under a "small contract.")

Flagstad's Isolde of April 12, 1941, turned out to be the soprano's last appearance at the House for nearly a decade. She wanted to retire and remain at home in Norway with her husband during the war years. Her retirement, however temporary, was only one of many wartime problems that beset the Johnson regime. Nevertheless, the Metropolitan came through the war years relatively unscathed. New European singers continued to be added to the roster, including Martial Singher, and the shortage of seasoned new talent provided opportunities for American singers such as Richard Tucker, Blanche Thebom, and Jerome Hines to develop their versatility in all areas of the repertory.

That repertory was not greatly expanded in the years of Johnson's management. Aside from *The Man Without a Country* —a viable, pleasant score that no one seemed to want back after a second season—only three operas were given their premieres between 1935 and 1950: Richard Hageman's *Caponsacchi,* which had been introduced five years earlier in Freiburg; Gian Carlo Menotti's *Island God*; and Bernard Rogers' *Warrior,* an experiment in musical theater that was quickly judged a poor risk for Metropolitan audiences.

There were a number of revivals, however, particularly in the French wing of the repertory. Lily Pons sang in a revival of *Le Coq d'Or* in 1937, the first in nine seasons, and Dorothy Kirsten sang the title role in *Louise* in 1947, in a memorial to the late Grace Moore. The German wing of the repertory saw three innovations during Johnson's management: *Hänsel und Gretel* in English, the first opera ever to be recorded in the House; Mozart's *Entführung aus dem Serail,* also in English, in its only Metropolitan season, 1946–1947; and in 1947–1948 a new production of *The Ring* with sets by Lee Simonson.

In retrospect, Johnson's greatest achievements as manager appear to be his engagement of major conductors, the popularization of Mozart, and the emphasis on Richard Strauss. Three Strauss operas were presented in a single season—1936–1937. *Der Rosenkavalier* was of course the great favorite; and one of the most nostalgic occasions of the Johnson era was the performance on February 23, 1945, when Lotte Lehmann bowed out as the Marschallin, a role she had made uniquely her own. But it must not be forgotten that she enjoyed the support of a well-rounded ensemble, largely of American singers—which may have been the greatest contribution of all that Edward Johnson made to the Metropolitan Opera.

First success of Johnson's first season: When the new general manager greeted Australian soprano Marjorie Lawrence after her debut as Brünnhilde in *Die Walküre (opposite),* he had reason to feel buoyant.

Three of Johnson's giants: The team of Flagstad and Melchior first kindled *Tristan und Isolde* on February 6, 1935, four days after the Norwegian soprano's debut. A couple of years later Giovanni Martinelli sang his first *Otello* at the Metropolitan, bringing Verdi's late opera back to popularity after an absence of a quarter-century; the production (*opposite, below,* Act III) was Donald Oenslager's.

Mainstays of the wartorn roster: Stars of the forties included German baritone Herbert Janssen (*left above,* as Telramund in *Lohengrin*) and Kerstin Thorborg, whose roles ranged from Marina in *Boris Godunov* (*below*) to Fricka, Amneris, and Dalila. Meanwhile, the unsung artists of the orchestra (*opposite page*) continued to supply first-rate support from the pit.

COLOR SPREAD:

One of the handsomest productions at the Opera House for twenty-five years was Willy Pogany's *Coq d'Or,* new in 1917–1918 and still on view in 1945, when Margaret Harshaw sang Amelfa and Norman Cordon the King.

New luster for Mozart and Wagner: During the latter half of Johnson's regime, *Don Giovanni* boasted the kind of ensemble shown on the opposite page—James Melton, Zinka Milanov, Bidù Sayão, Jarmila Novotna, Ezio Pinza, and Salvatore Baccaloni—and the roles Kirsten Flagstad had vacated were filled by Missouri-born Helen Traubel (*left,* as Elisabeth in *Tannhäuser*).

Pearl Harbor and Nagasaki: Following the news of December 7, 1941, Puccini's *Madama Butterfly* made no further appearances at the Metropolitan until 1946, when the Japanese heroine was again sung by Licia Albanese (*opposite page*). Meanwhile, for the duration, military headgear vied with top hats in the Opera House cloakrooms.

The press photographer comes into his own:
During the forties, the diamonds of Mrs.
George Washington Kavanaugh and her friend
Lady Decies brightened the institution of
opening night; tabloid cameraman Weegee
recorded this historic confrontation by the
curb (*opposite page*), but his less imaginative
colleagues awaited their quarry in the
Thirty-ninth Street lobby.

Opera as Theater
1950–1966

While increasing attention was being paid to décor at the Metropolitan, stage direction had not kept pace. It remained for Rudolf Bing, an Austrian trained in Germany, to remind the ageless lady of seventy that she was located, after all, on Broadway. The new general manager's emphasis on theater was reflected in improvements made to the building in the summer of 1953. These included reseating of the Orchestra and removal of the antiquated Orchestra Circle—the last horseshoe but one, in which people faced not the stage but each other across the auditorium. The hundred displaced standees were provided for in the Balcony, and the Orchestra seats added were arranged to give increased visibility. By assuring as many customers as he could a direct view of the stage and not of each other, the new general manager appeared to be underscoring his determination to produce operas worthy of being seen as well as heard.

Rudolf Bing's devotion to drama was without parallel. With the possible exception of Heinrich Conried, former managers had been preoccupied only with the musical quality of a production. Before the mid-thirties, and the end of the old "star" system, the dramatic aspects of the Metropolitan Opera were attended to almost exclusively by one or two overworked stage directors such as Wilhelm von Wymetal, who was intermittently with the Company from 1922 to 1936. The idea of importing a specialist had occurred to the management only in the case of David Belasco, though earlier an arrangement had been made outside the Company in presenting the works of Wagner. The German composer had started a European tradition by becoming his own stage director, and at the Metropolitan he was represented by disciples from the Bayreuth circle, notably Wilhelm Hock (who directed a production of *Die Walküre* in 1885) and Anton Fuchs, who was responsible for the *Parsifal* and *Meistersinger* of the 1903–1904 season.

The choice of David Belasco to stage the two Puccini operas based on his own plays—*Madama Butterfly* (1907) and *La Fanciulla del West* (1910)—was an obvious one, but ten years later the management called on Belasco again to stage Leoncavallo's *Zazà,* in which Geraldine Farrar was starred. The colorful Belasco (whose habit of wearing a clerical collar earned him the monicker "Bishop of Broadway") helped to make the first *Fanciulla* the success it was, his accomplishments on that occasion including

"making the singers act and the chorus stand still. Destinn had to sing while serving drinks, Caruso while climbing a ladder."

The Metropolitan Opera's first stage director officially listed as such appears to have been Richard Ordynski, who in 1917 handled the premiere of De Koven's *Canterbury Pilgrims.* Few other stage directors made news until 1929, when Ernst Lert, who had worked with Toscanini at La Scala, declared that the "three or four rehearsals" he was given to mount a Metropolitan revival of *Fanciulla* were quite inadequate. Happier with their lot were Désiré Defrère, who started directing in 1934–1935 after twenty seasons as a baritone, and Leopold Sachse, whom Edward Johnson engaged in his first season to pump new life into *Tristan und Isolde* and later into *Der Fliegende Holländer.*

Both Defrère and Sachse stayed on, as did Herbert Graf, another Johnson import. When Graf, the son of a leading Viennese music critic, arrived at the Opera House in 1936 he brought with him not only interesting theories but practical stage experience; this he had gained in Breslau, in Moscow with Konstantin Stanislavski, and more especially in Salzburg, where he had worked with Toscanini and Bruno Walter. In quick succession Graf was assigned *Samson et Dalila, Les Contes d'Hoffmann, Salome, Falstaff, Orfeo ed Euridice,* and, in 1940, *Le Nozze di Figaro.* The following season he staged the Metropolitan premiere of Gluck's *Alceste,* and as recently as 1963 he collaborated with Eugene Berman on a new *Otello.* Apart from Lothar Wallerstein, who in 1942 asked that his name be removed from the program of *Die Walküre,* and Dino Yannopoulos, a Graf student who made his debut directing *Il Tabarro* in 1946, there was little more of note in the history of Metropolitan stage direction until Rudolf Bing arrived in 1950. The traditional shrines had been Bayreuth and Salzburg and, with the sole exception of Belasco, the Broadway showmen working within a few blocks of the Opera House during the twenties, thirties, and forties had all been completely ignored.

In *Don Carlo,* the performance which opened Bing's initial season on November 6, 1950, there were five debuts: those of Fedora Barbieri, Delia Rigal, and Cesare Siepi onstage, Rolf Gérard in the role of designer, and Margaret Webster as director. The name of Miss Webster came last alphabetically but certainly not least in the eyes of the critics. For a new *Fledermaus,* presented a month later, Bing had chosen Garson Kanin to stage the opera with a "revised" book and an English translation by Howard Dietz. The refurbished Johann Strauss operetta became the greatest box-office success to date. During the next few years Bing

---

The last complete role sung by Leonard Warren before his death on the Metropolitan stage (March 4, 1960) was Verdi's Simon Boccanegra, whose climactic moment he enacts opposite (Ezio Flagello as Paolo).

The last word on *Simon Boccanegra:* A 1959–1960 revival of Verdi's Genoese opera enlisted the services of Margaret Webster as director (*opposite page, above,* demonstrating a sword thrust), Dimitri Mitropoulos as conductor (*below,* going over a passage with Leonard Warren and Giorgio Tozzi), and a distinguished cast, among them Mary Curtis-Verna and Richard Tucker, shown at left rehearsing their third-act ensemble.

Preparing a performance: Rehearsals at the Opera House take place all over—in the Guild Room (*opposite page, above,* Rosalind Elias and Franco Corelli preparing *Andrea Chénier*), on the roof stage (*below,* Franco Zeffirelli and Martin Rich coaching Messrs. Macurdy, Graham, and Sereni in *Falstaff*), and on the main stage (*left,* Cyril Ritchard pacing Judith Raskin and Elfego Esparza in *Le Nozze di Figaro*).

invited Alfred Lunt to direct *Così Fan Tutte* (in an English translation by Ruth and Thomas Martin), Tyrone Guthrie from London to direct *Carmen,* and Joseph Mankiewicz from Hollywood to direct *La Bohème.* The international gamut eventually ran from Aoyama to Zeffirelli, encompassing on the way George Balanchine (*The Rake's Progress*), Carl Ebert (*Macbeth*), Gian Carlo Menotti (*Vanessa* and his own *Last Savage*), José Quintero (*Cavalleria Rusticana* and *Pagliacci*), and Günther Rennert (*Un Ballo in Maschera* and *Salome*), among others. At least three of these directors—Miss Webster, the Messrs. Ebert and Lunt—had been actors themselves, and with them drama came to the Opera House to stay.

With it came scenic design of a strikingly theatrical kind. Whether in the Piranesi-like prison of *Don Carlo* (designed by Rolf Gérard) or the candy-box packaging of *Martha* (by Oliver Smith), style was the prevailing concern. The Middle European discipline of Caspar Neher's designs for *Macbeth* (matched by the direction of Ebert, who succeeded in making the chorus hold still) was merged with the movement and ease of the popular stage, as in *Fledermaus.* Announcing that "my management . . . will attempt to adapt the scenic, dramatic, and visual aspects [of opera] to more contemporary lines," Bing nevertheless tried only one out-and-out experimental production: the *Cavalleria* and *Pagliacci* of his maiden season, designed by Horace Armistead. Other, more circumspect productions introduced modern techniques, however, as in *Parsifal,* which had scenic projections designed by Leo Kerz and brought the Company as far as it has come to date in the direction of Bayreuth staging as evolved by Wagner's grandsons.

In *La Traviata* (1956–1957), the Metropolitan took a bold leap from Bayreuth back to Broadway. Oliver Smith, who had done settings for ballet and musical comedy, designed the production in a highly personal style, and Tyrone Guthrie took the cue for his "choreographic" staging from the dance rhythms that pervade Verdi's score. The Bing management has employed other major designers: Berman (*Rigoletto, Don Giovanni, La Forza del Destino, Otello*), Cecil Beaton (*Vanessa, Turandot*), Beni Montresor (*The Last Savage*), Robert O'Hearn (*Aida, Die Meistersinger, Samson et Dalila, L'Elisir d'Amore, Pique Dame*), and Ita Maximowna (*Un Ballo in Maschera, Manon*). More recently, as in Attilio Colonnello's *Lucia di Lammermoor* and Franco Zeffirelli's *Falstaff,* it has also brought into American focus the current European trend—re-establishment of the opera's own period and heavily detailed, rather literal settings drafted with high style.

The elaborate sets and costumes that went to make up each new production in Bing's repertory added to the mounting costs. To help meet these, the management with businesslike dispatch doubled the ticket prices for opening night, raised them for the "popular-priced" Saturday-night subscription series, and added a new Tuesday series to bring additional income. Bing also tightened the Door List, a dispensation by which hangers-on had poured into the Opera House by the back way without paying admission.

The Metropolitan's long-standing income from piano endorsements (since 1926, the Knabe), from recorded performances, and from radio sponsorship (since 1940, Texaco) had been supplemented by three televised openings: *Otello* in 1948, *Der Rosenkavalier* in 1949, and *Don Carlo* in 1950. Bing now turned a receptive ear to bids from closed-circuit television, and on December 11, 1952, a regular performance on the new Guthrie *Carmen* was shown to paying audiences in twenty-seven cities from coast to coast.

That same season Graf oversaw specially prepared studio-TV performances of *Fledermaus* and *La Bohème* (also translated by Howard Dietz). All these experiments were successful, but none realized such steady support as the National Council of the Metropolitan Opera, which Mrs. Belmont organized in 1952 as a means of securing the participation of local leaders on a nationwide basis.

Unlike Gatti and Johnson, Rudolf Bing in his first years risked no novelty by an American composer, unless Igor Stravinsky can be considered in this category. The American premiere of *The Rake's Progress,* conducted by Fritz Reiner on Valentine's Day, 1953, was a success at first, less so subsequently. As his tenure became more secure, Bing broadened the scope of the Metropolitan repertory to include Barber's *Vanessa* in 1958 and Berg's *Wozzeck* in 1959 (at the age of thirty-four, a dubious "novelty"), but audiences were not especially receptive. Adjusting his sights to the more conservative taste of the Opera's most faithful customers, the general manager planned a more balanced repertory and arranged for more operas to be sung in English.

In 1953 *Boris Godunov* was revived successfully in a new translation by John Gutman. Gutman also provided the English text for Richard Strauss's *Arabella,* seen by American audiences

These stars of the first magnitude were in conjunction the night of November 29, 1964, for the Guild's Welfare-Pension Fund benefit—Joan Sutherland, Renata Tebaldi, Elisabeth Schwarzkopf, Lisa Della Casa.

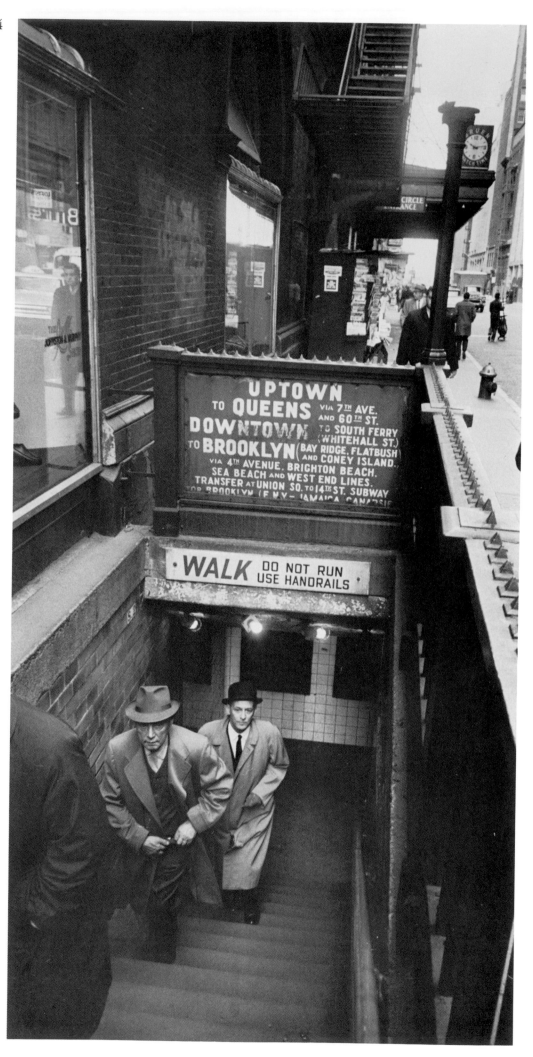

Subway to the Met: "Mr. Bing," as he is known to all and sundry around the Opera House, rides to it democratically (*left*), works autocratically, and relaxes diplomatically (*opposite page, above,* with Roger Seydoux, French ambassador to the United Nations, in his box before a performance). When he does take a break for lunch, it is usually combined with business (*below,* discussing *The Last Savage* with Gian Carlo Menotti).

Dictators of the baton: Among recent maestros who have brought out the best in the Metropolitan Opera Orchestra are the Austrian Karl Boehm (*opposite page, above*), the Hungarian Georg Solti (*below*), and the young American Thomas Schippers (*left*).

Building a ballet company: Steps toward the goal of raising the Metropolitan's corps of dancers to equal status with its roster of singers have included the engagement of guest choreographers for dance sequences in opera (*opposite page*, Todd Bolender devising the Dance of the Apprentices for *Die Meistersinger*) and the building of an independent dance repertory under new ballet director Alicia Markova (*left*, coaching Hans Meister in *Les Sylphides*).

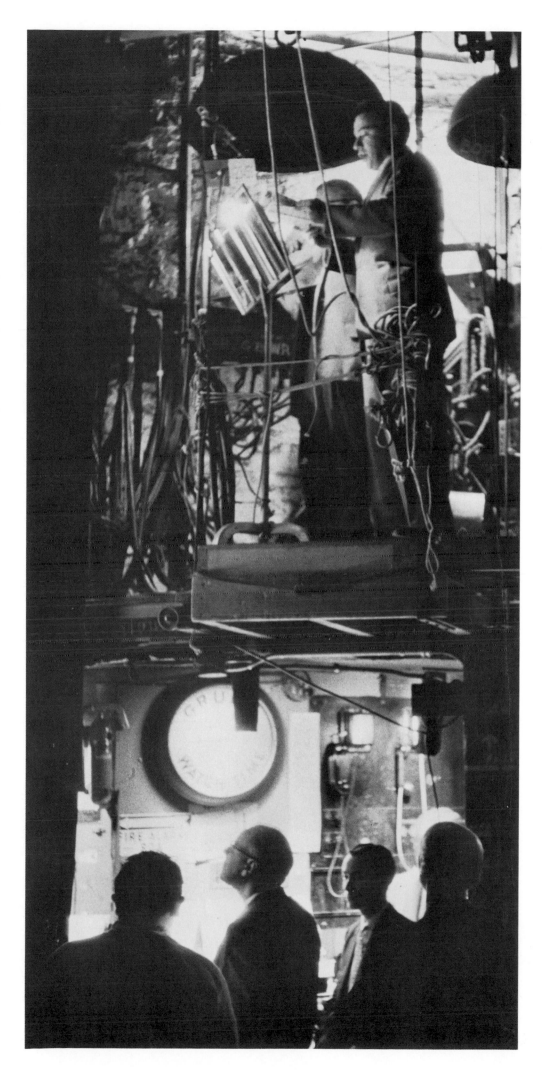

The unsung specialists backstage: Orchestra manager Felix Eyle coordinates a rehearsal of Strauss's demanding *Ariadne auf Naxos* (*opposite page, above*); next to the fire door that separates the stage from backstage, assistant conductor Julius Burger and associate stage manager Stanley Levine take time out to enjoy (and clock) a performance (*below*). At left, Charles Anthony sings the offstage sailor's song in Act I of *Tristan und Isolde* under the watchful gaze of general manager Bing (at right) and his colleagues.

Behind the scenes: Eavesdroppers backstage at the Metropolitan may find Cesare Siepi gargling before his entrance as Don Giovanni or, on another night, choristers returning from their stint onstage in *Ernani*.

for the first time in 1955. Tchaikovsky's *Eugene Onegin* returned to the Metropolitan in 1957 and was sung in English to an apathetic opening-night audience.

In addition Bing chose and polished up other scores that the public had almost forgotten. *Così Fan Tutte* had been absent twenty-three seasons when Bing revived it in 1951, *Don Carlo* and *Ernani* twenty-seven, and *Fledermaus* forty-four. *Macbeth* and *Nabucco,* never given before at the Metropolitan, received mixed notices in the press when they were sung in 1959 and 1960, respectively; with *Ernani,* however, they slowly won a public for the early Verdi.

Faust, on the other hand, which had opened the house in 1883–1884 and had hardly been absent for a season since, had grown stale through the years, and Bing refurbished it for the 1953–1954 season. The production, directed by the Old Vic's Peter Brook, boldly broke with tradition. Rolf Gérard changed the setting to a university town of the mid-nineteenth century and outfitted Méphistophélès, sung by Nicola Rossi-Lemeni, in an opera cloak, top hat, and cane. Jussi Bjoerling, Victoria de los Angeles, and Robert Merrill were also in the cast, and Pierre Monteux conducted, at the opening-night performance on November 16. The controversy that followed hurt box-office receipts not at all.

Also planned within the first week of that season were four memorable debuts: Lisa Della Casa as the Countess and Irmgard Seefried as Susanna in *Le Nozze di Figaro,* Josef Metternich as Don Carlo in *La Forza del Destino,* and James McCracken, a great Otello-to-be, as Parpignol in *La Bohème.* In line with the Metropolitan's new policy, most of these stars proved reliable actors as well as expert singers. Later seasons produced more of the same. Other stars from abroad who have added luster to the Metropolitan firmament include Mario Del Monaco, Hilde Gueden, Ettore Bastianini, Fernando Corena, Otto Edelmann, Renata Tebaldi, Tito Gobbi, Antonietta Stella, Nicolai Gedda, Mario Sereni, Leonie Rysanek, Giulietta Simionato, Birgit Nilsson, Jon Vickers, Gabriella Tucci, Franco Corelli, Joan Sutherland, Rita Gorr, Régine Crespin, Luigi Alva, Elisabeth Schwarzkopf, and Bruno Prevedi.

Among the Americans to have risen under Bing's aegis are Roberta Peters, Lucine Amara, Mildred Miller, Nell Rankin, Rosalind Elias, Giorgio Tozzi, Ezio Flagello, Mignon Dunn, Barry Morell, and Teresa Stratas. There have been other Americans who won success elsewhere before joining the Metropolitan—George London, Maria Callas, Irene Dalis, Mary Curtis-Verna, Cornell MacNeil, Anna Moffo, Eileen Farrell, William Dooley, Gianna d'Angelo, John Alexander, Judith Raskin, Jess Thomas. Meanwhile, Marian Anderson, the first Negro to sing with the Company (on January 7, 1955, as Ulrica in *Un Ballo in Maschera*), opened the doors to such artists as Leontyne Price, Mattiwilda Dobbs, George Shirley, Gloria Davy, and Martina Arroyo.

Mr. Bing had his problems too, however. There were pickets on hand when, during his first season (1950–1951), Kirsten Flagstad returned to the Metropolitan from Norway, where she had spent the war years; she had already been cleared by the courts of her native land, but Edward Johnson had refused to sign her. There were also pickets to protest the "anticlericalism" of *Don Carlo* when Verdi's opera, which had opened the season, was repeated. Bing championed the work nevertheless, and the pickets disappeared.

Twice during his regime (August 1961 and October 1964) the season was actually canceled, owing to inability to reach agreement with labor unions over a contract; but both times the season went on. Such difficulties did not prevent Bing from encouraging improvements in the Metropolitan chorus, carried out under chorus master Kurt Adler, and in the ballet, which has been developing its own individuality under Antony Tudor, Zachary Solov, and especially its latest director, Dame Alicia Markova. Conductors who have appeared at the Metropolitan first under Bing include Dimitri Mitropoulos, Leopold Stokowski, Leonard Bernstein, Karl Boehm, and Thomas Schippers.

As if to sum up these fifteen successful years, a gala *Tosca* on March 19, 1965 (featuring Callas, Corelli, and Gobbi) showed public approval by selling out months in advance. And for the final season in the old Opera House it was arranged to open with yet another production of *Faust,* staged by Jean-Louis Barrault.

As operagoers took their seats around the edge of the Orchestra for that performance, only the row of boxes directly above their heads would remain unchanged from the original Opera House of 1883. But not for nothing was it called the Golden Horseshoe—it had always been composed of the most enduring metal.

One of the most sensational events ever to take place at the Metropolitan was the debut of of Maria Callas as Norma (shown opposite with Mario Del Monaco) on the opening night of the 1956–1957 season.

Confrontations tragic and comic: Highlights of
recent Metropolitan seasons have included
Franco Corelli and Robert Merrill in the trial
scene of Giordano's *Andrea Chénier* (*left*),
Anselmo Colzani and Gabriella Tucci in the
rendezvous scene of Verdi's *Falstaff* (*opposite
page, above*), and Leontyne Price repulsing
Cornell MacNeil in Act I of the same
composer's *Ernani.*

COLOR SPREAD:

The *Turandot* cast has its picture taken: Highlight of the 1960–1961 season was Cecil Beaton's new production of the posthumous Puccini opera, in which conductor Leopold Stokowski made his debut with the Company. Here, ranged across the Act II, Scene 2 set are Charles Anthony, Frank Guarrera, Robert Nagy, Birgit Nilsson, Franco Corelli, Bonaldo Giaiotti, Anna Moffo, and (on the throne) Alessio De Paolis.

Prima donnas of Italian opera: Joan Sutherland (*opposite page, above,* with John Alexander) starred in a new production of Donizetti's *Lucia di Lammermoor,* designed by Attilio Colonnello and staged by Margherita Wallmann, which opened the 1964–1965 Metropolitan season; Maria Callas returned to the Opera House that same season for two sensational *Tosca*s (*below,* with Tito Gobbi). Meanwhile, American soprano Mary Costa had made her debut as Violetta in *La Traviata* (*left*) and later starred in Samuel Barber's *Vanessa.*

Great entrances in *opera buffa*: Dr. Dulcamara's arrival in a balloon, as provided by designer Robert O'Hearn and director Nathaniel Merrill in their 1960 production of *L'Elisir d'Amore* (*opposite page*), was paralleled by Abdul's arrival in a cage in Gian Carlo Menotti's *Last Savage,* designed by Beni Montresor in 1964 and staged by the composer. While the musical inspiration, too, was similar, it cannot be said that Fernando Corena's impersonation bore much resemblance to that of George London (*left,* surrounded by Teresa Stratas, Ezio Flagello, Lili Chookasian, Roberta Peters, Nicolai Gedda, Morley Meredith).

A credit to Shakespeare: Verdi's *Macbeth* is one of several established works never heard at the Metropolitan before Rudolf Bing staged them. The 1959 production, designed by Caspar Neher and directed by Carl Ebert, reached its climax in the scene of Banquo's ghost, when Macbeth (*left,* Cornell MacNeil) alone was in hallucinated motion against a chorus that remained largely motionless in pale garb and make-up.

Two ladies from Philadelphia: When Marian Anderson (*left*) made her debut as Ulrica in *Un Ballo in Maschera,* on January 7, 1955, it was the first time a Negro had sung a solo role at the Metropolitan. When Anna Moffo (*opposite page*) made her debut as Violetta in another Verdi opera, *La Traviata,* it was as an American girl who had won her first laurels in Italy, studying on a Fulbright grant.

The American singer comes into his own: Memorable characterizations of recent years have included Farrell as La Gioconda in Ponchielli's opera (*left*), James McCracken as Verdi's Otello (*below,* with Gabriella Tucci) and Dorothy Kirsten's Cio-Cio-San (*opposite page,* with John Alexander in Act I of *Madama Butterfly*).

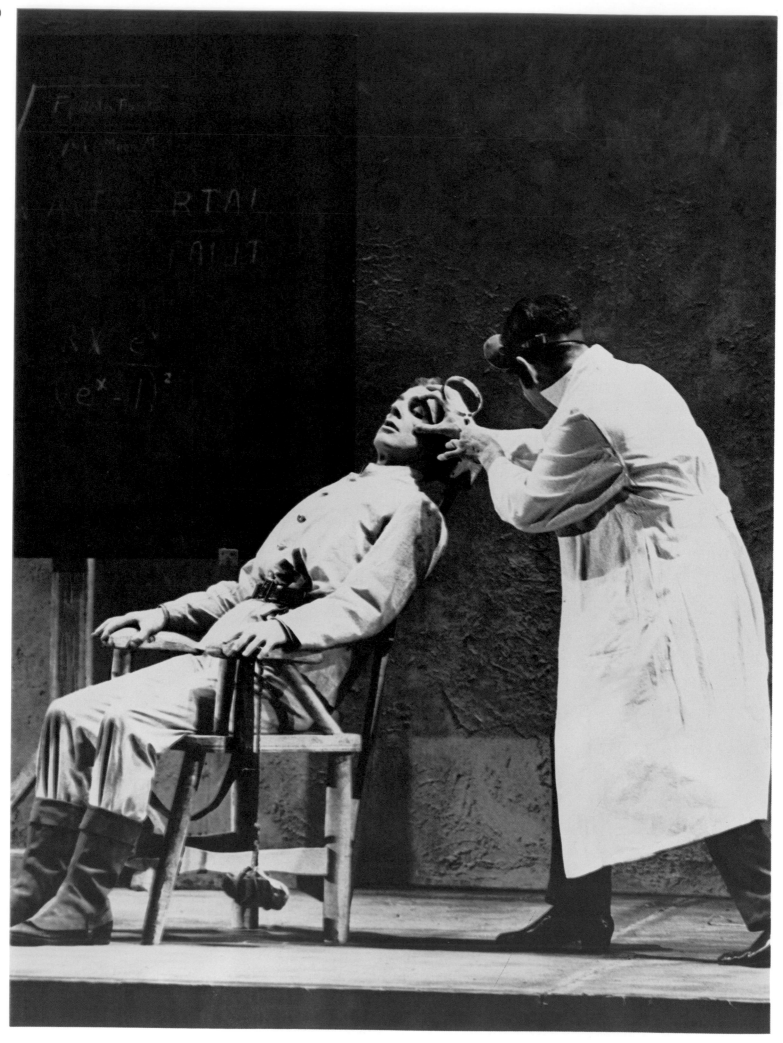

Music drama and operetta: The Metropolitan premiere of *Wozzeck,* one of its most highly regarded efforts, took place in 1959 after some forty rehearsals and featured Hermann Uhde as the hero (*opposite page,* with Ralph Herbert as the mad Doctor). Another Bing specialty has been operetta translated into English, such as Offenbach's *Perichole* (*left,* with Patrice Munsel and Theodor Uppman) and Johann Strauss's *Fledermaus* (*below,* Frank Guarrera as Dr. Falke, the "bat").

Twentieth-century music drama: One of the most distinguished of Opera House collaborations came with a new *Salome* on February 3, 1965—staged by Günther Rennert, designed in Art Nouveau-expressionistic style by Rudolf Heinrich, conducted by Karl Boehm, and sung by Birgit Nilsson in the title role (shown opposite, with Irene Dalis, in the Dance of the Seven Veils, at left in the finale).

On April 5, 1965, Verdi's *Aida*—the most popular opera at the Metropolitan—attained its 500th performance there. The previous season it had been accorded a sumptuous new production by O'Hearn and Merrill, with "ethnic" choreography by Katherine Dunham; in the Triumphal Scene, Radames was borne in standing upon a litter (here, Richard Tucker, John Macurdy).

Great ladies of operatic comedy: Elisabeth Schwarzkopf is shown opposite, bowing after her debut as the Marschallin in *Der Rosenkavalier*. The bored soprano on the swing is Victoria de los Angeles as Lady Harriet, alias "Martha," in Oliver Smith's production of the Flotow comic opera, with Lorenzo Alvary as Tristram.

The "total work of art": This was what Wagner asked of his Muse, and this is what he has received increasingly at the Opera House. Who can forget Leonie Rysanek as Senta in *Der Fliegende Holländer* (*opposite page, above*), Birgit Nilsson and Ramon Vinay as Isolde and Tristan (*below*), or (*left*) the gathering of the vassals around Ernst Wiemann as Hagen in *Götterdämmerung?*

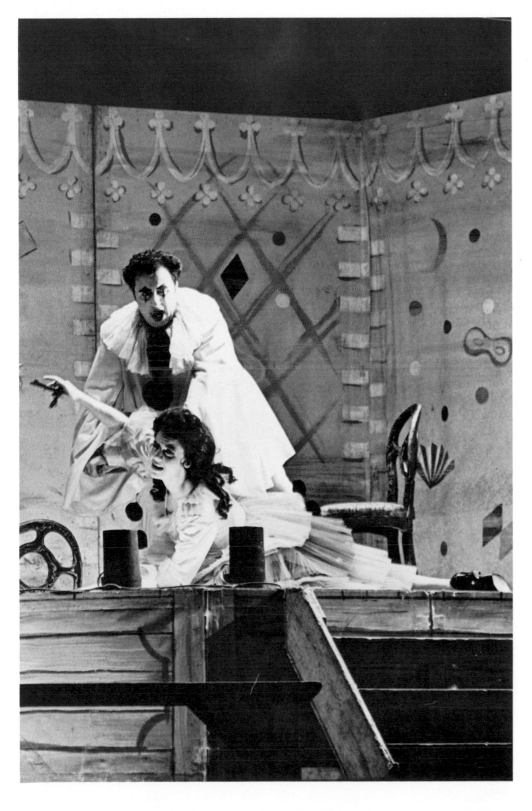

Larger than life: Some of the most popular personalities in recent Metropolitan history have specialized in the late-romantic Italian repertory, such as Renata Tebaldi (*opposite page,* as the heroine of Cilèa's *Adriana Lecouvreur,* which was revived for her in 1963). Another melodrama about actors is *Pagliacci,* recently performed at the Metropolitan by Carlo Bergonzi and Raina Kabaivanska (*left*).

Prize Song for a prize *Meistersinger*: One of
the most acclaimed productions of the Bing
regime was the one devised for Wagner's lone
comedy by designer Robert O'Hearn and
director Nathaniel Merrill during the
1962–1963 season. When Sándor Kónya as
Walther delivered his Prize Song in Act III,
before a circle of red-cloaked Mastersingers on
one side and the whole panorama of
Nuremberg on the other, many felt that a
triumph had indeed been scored. (At right,
Ezio Flagello and Ingrid Bjoner.)

Three faces of French opera: Risë Stevens'
impersonation of Carmen (*opposite, left,* with
Mmes. Amara and Roggero, Messrs. De Paolis
and Cehanovsky) was one reason Bizet's work
remained the most popular at the Metropolitan
after *Aida* and *La Bohème.* Spokesmen for
other areas of Gallic lyric theater have included
Jess Thomas (*opposite,* pushing the mill
wheel) in Saint-Saëns' *Samson et Dalila,* and
Anna Moffo (*left,* with Frank Guarrera as her
cousin) in Massenet's *Manon.*

The comic and touching sides of Strauss: The latest undisputed master of opera has been treated well at the Metropolitan, particularly in the casts lavished on his *Rosenkavalier*. Here we see Lynn Owen, Anneliese Rothenberger, and Lisa Della Casa in the Presentation of the Silver Rose (*opposite, above*), Régine Crespin and Hertha Töpper at the end of the first act (*below*), Rosalind Elias and Otto Edelmann at the end of the second.

The finished performance: After weeks of planning and hours of strenuous rehearsal, a ballet such as the Metropolitan's 1964–1965 *Sylphides* is unveiled before the audience. Here, Hans Meister lifts Katharyn Horne to the opening strains of Chopin's Nocturne in E-flat, while the *corps* sustains a poetic pose.

High spirits in the dressing room: When the tension of performance is past, the artists can be themselves. Here are candid shots of Lisa Della Casa removing her hat after singing Donna Elvira in the first act of *Don Giovanni*, and Jan Peerce congratulating Mattiwilda Dobbs after their performance of *Rigoletto*, in which she made her Metropolitan debut.

Galas for charity and for champions: The Welfare Fund benefit on December 14, 1960, included a concert against the second-act setting from Strauss's *Arabella*; among the performers was Licia Albanese, who sang an aria from Boito's *Mefistofele* (*opposite page*). General manager Rudolf Bing stepped into the spotlight for Kirsten Flagstad's farewell in 1952 (*below, after Alcestis*) and for Zinka Milanov's twenty-fifth anniversary *Chénier* in 1962 (*left*).

Top Hats on the Grand Tier: Evening dress is still the order of the day in the Metropolitan Opera Club, whose members fill their portion of the Grand Tier with stag elegance on Monday evenings. They also have a club room for the pause that refreshes during intermission.

The grandeur that is opera: On gala evenings, the Metropolitan still captures some of the aura traditionally associated with its fabled past, enhanced by the presence of such personalities as Leonard Bernstein and Adlai Stevenson (*opposite,* at a dinner before the World's Fair season of 1964) and Mrs. John F. Kennedy, shown at left arriving for the *Tosca* benefit of 1965.

The gallery of the gods: It has been said that the "true" opera-lover can be found in the Family Circle, topmost of the Metropolitan's six levels. For $1.50 the young can buy standing room directly beneath the ornate gilt ceiling (*opposite page*); for $2.50 they may stand in the Orchestra. For outstanding events, all such tickets involve long waits in line (*left*), whereas the average operagoer does not arrive until curtain time.

Epilogue

BY ANTHONY A. BLISS

Though in the course of things the building came first, before there was any Metropolitan Opera Company, yet the single-purposed objective of those vigorous men of the 1880's who built it was the Company that has now flourished these fourscore years.

We of the 1960's are, in a very real sense, trustees pledged to continuing the dedicated ideal of these music-minded pioneers, the ideal of a resident opera company serving the public with performances of the highest quality man's ever increasing genius can make possible.

So, in the course of things and of eighty-three years, our Metropolitan Opera Company has grown with the times to maintain and even surpass the magnificent performance levels of its early seasons. It is at least the peer of any opera company in the world. (We, in all modesty, consider it without peer.) But in our age of prodigies in technical advance, the House that has been home to the Metropolitan Opera Company all these years has—for many and weighty reasons beyond solution—become less serviceable, a less economically and esthetically practical instrument for maintaining and improving performance quality and public service. From 1908 on, step by step in the pages of this volume, has been recorded the growing need for a new opera house, stated publicly by Gatti-Casazza and Otto Kahn back in 1924. Had both a major depression and a world war not intervened, there is little question: the Metropolitan Opera would have had a new home many years ago.

Now the inevitable moment has arrived, with its harmonics born of anticipation for a superb new opera house and of sadness in bidding farewell to a beautiful and distinguished auditorium of cherished memories.

But the masterpiece of literature must outlive its binding, and the song must outlive both the singer and the lute. In the world of theater the show must not only go on, it must go forward and upward with each successive improvement in technology and audience comfort. The monumental new Metropolitan Opera House at Lincoln Center will be a fitting instrument for perhaps a century of performances, excitingly able to fulfill the ideals of the Metropolitan's founders, who dreamed extravagant dreams and made them come true. Their bequest to us is the finest opera company on earth.

We salute the future with confidence and enthusiasm as we too dream—of the prodigies of production, of the expanded service to artists and public alike, and of the enrichment of opera in America made possible by the new home of the Metropolitan Opera.

Encore:

Distinguished Guests

Six nights a week—Monday through Saturday—in the season, the Metropolitan Opera House is a blaze of lights, as grand opera with all the trimmings is performed by the resident Company. On the seventh night, and between seasons, the house is dark, except on those occasions when it becomes a showcase for visiting artists appearing under auspices other than those of the Metropolitan. The House has served, on occasion, as a concert hall, recital hall, lecture hall, even as a legitimate theater. Many of those who perform there do not a utter a note of music, though Bernard Shaw, speaking on April 11, 1933, as guest of the Academy of Political Science, on "The Future of Political Science in America," did observe that he felt an almost uncontrollable urge to sing.

For the first sixty years of its life, the Metropolitan's management solved the problem of how to keep the House in use every night of the week without violating the taboo on Sabbath "theatricals" by making it available for Sunday-night concerts. The League of Composers also was responsible for a memorable series of events: between 1929 and 1935 six new or little-known operas, by Stravinsky, Shostakovich, and others, were given their New York premieres in staged versions, a number of them by the Philadelphia Orchestra under Leopold Stokowski.

The great impresario of ballet at the Metropolitan has been Sol Hurok, who has brought the foremost dancers and ballet companies to the Opera House for spring and fall seasons, beginning with Isadora Duncan in 1916. Hurok brought De Basil's Ballets Russes de Monte Carlo to the Metropolitan in 1935. Ballet Theatre followed in 1942, and in 1949 Hurok imported the London Sadler's Wells Ballet, which scored an instant success—as did Moscow's spectacular Bolshoi Ballet in 1959.

The most illustrious actress of her day, Eleonora Duse, stepped upon the stage in October 1923, when she was sixty-four, to play Ibsen's *Lady from the Sea*. Much earlier, in 1888, the eminent Shakespeareans Edwin Booth and Helena Modjeska starred there in a five-act performance of *Hamlet*. Sarah Bernhardt, Mrs. Patrick Campbell, Maude Adams, Ethel Barrymore, even such popular entertainers as Lillian Russell, Sir Harry Lauder, George M. Cohan, and the comedians Weber and Fields, have graced the stage. The Metropolitan even housed a suffrage pageant, in which Lillian Nordica, as Columbia, shared the limelight with ex-President Theodore Roosevelt, as himself.

Edward Steichen's portrait of Leopold Stokowski (1928) shows the conductor of the Philadelphia Orchestra at the height of his powers, a year before his first appearance at the Metropolitan Opera House.

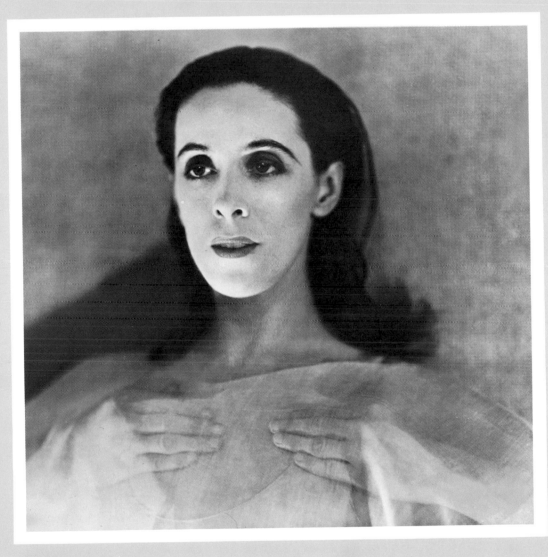

The chosen virgin: When the League of Composers presented the American stage premiere of *Le Sacre du Printemps,* Stravinsky's pagan ballet, at the Metropolitan on April 22, 1930, the soloist was a young American dancer with a great future, Martha Graham. (She would also appear on the opening bill at Radio City Music Hall, December 27, 1932.) A climactic moment from Nicholas Roerich's production, choreographed by Massine, is shown opposite.

Berg and Stravinsky: Two of the twentieth century's most important lyric dramas had their New York premieres at the Opera House under joint auspices of the League of Composers and the Philadelphia Orchestra, Leopold Stokowski conducting. Alban Berg's *Wozzeck* reached the Metropolitan on November 24, 1931 (*opposite page above*, Robert Edmond Jones' nightmare set); Igor Stravinsky's *Oedipus Rex* had preceded it by seven months (*below*, Jones's oversize puppets, which mimed the action while Margarete Matzenauer and Paul Althouse sang). On April 25, 1929—six months ahead of the stock-market crash—the League had presented the American premiere of Stravinsky's ballet *Les Noces* (*left*, Valentina Kashouba and George Volodin as bride and groom).

Thespians on the lyric stage: Great actors and actresses who have performed at the Metropolitan include Helena Modjeska (*opposite page,* as "Magda") and Edwin Booth (*far left*), with whom she played a five-act *Hamlet* on May 21, 1888; Maude Adams (*left*), who played Joan of Arc at a tribute to Marshal Joffre in April 1917; Lawrence Barrett, seen as Othello to Booth's Iago in January 1889 (*below, left*); and Sir Herbert Beerbohm Tree, shown below, right, as Svengali in *Trilby,* which he offered as part of a war-relief benefit on April 17, 1917.

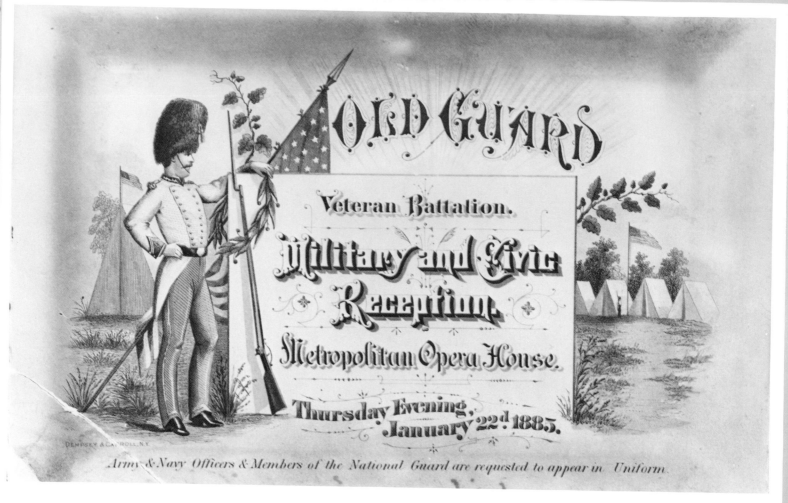

Veterans and vaudeville: If the several gatherings of the Old Guard (New York State Militia) must have brightened the Opera House with military colors, other offerings must have made its rafters ring with guffaws. The blackface trio shown on the opposite page— "W. Sweatnam, John Hart, Emil Ames"—took part in a minstrel show during the nineties; the pair on this page are Weber and Fields, who shared a 1912 bill with Al Jolson, Lillian Nordica, and the Dolly Sisters. Charity was the cause of these nonoperatic appearances, but the aim of the "Theatrical Business Men's Club" (*opposite page, below*) was clearly pleasure.

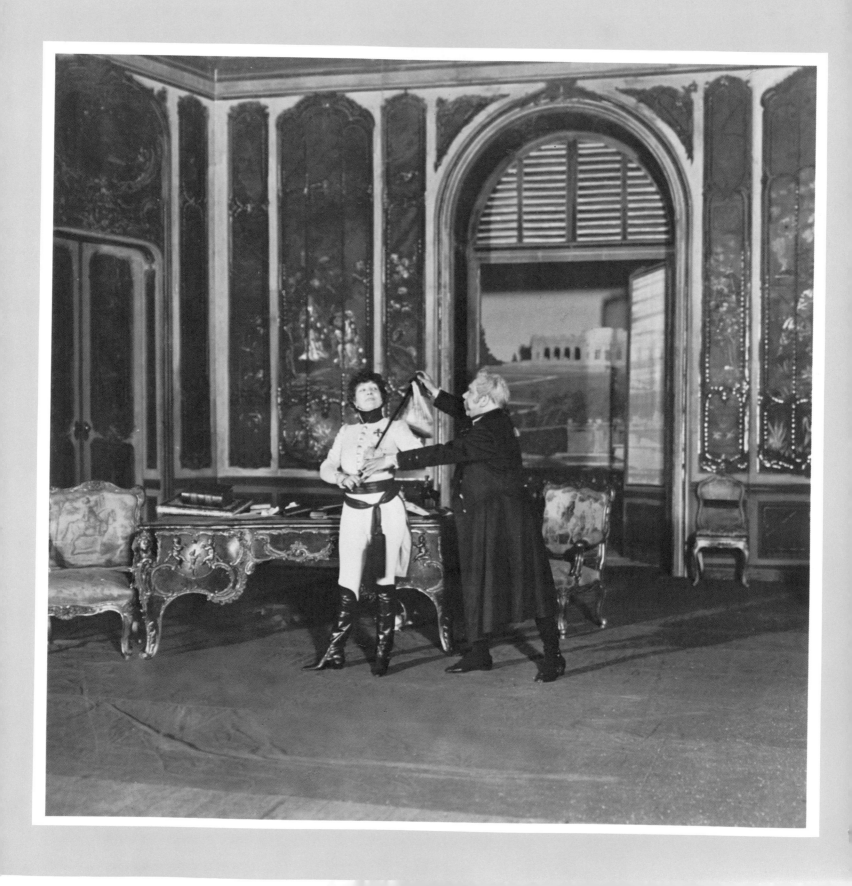

Bernhardt and Duse at the Metropolitan: In April 1892 the Divine Sarah gave a "Positively Farewell Appearance in America" as Sardou's Fedora, recently the subject of an opera by Giordano; but as late as April 1917 she played a scene from *Trilby* with Sir Herbert Beerbohm Tree. (*Opposite page:* Bernhardt in *L'Aiglon,* Rostand's play.) In October 1923 Eleonora Duse, frail at sixty-four, stepped upon the yawning stage to play Ibsen's *Lady from the Sea* in Italian; she died a few months later in Pittsburgh.

Distinguished Guests all: This grab-bag unites the Dolly Sisters; President Theodore Roosevelt, who spoke at a suffrage pageant; Admiral Richard E. Byrd, who lectured on his trips to the Pole (1930); John Philip Sousa, leader of his band on November 6, 1910; Marie Tempest, who performed on a bill of February 11, 1892; Victor Herbert, a cellist in the Opera House orchestra who lived to see two of his operas performed there; Sir Harry Lauder, a 1918 visitor; and Ethel Barrymore, who acted in several benefits.

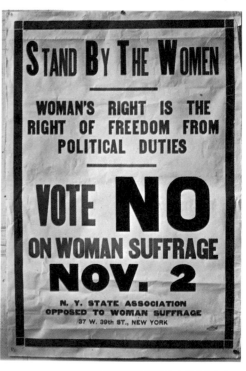

Disagreement on the rights of women: While suffragettes were stumping the city streets (*opposite page*), Lillian Nordica was singing her last—"The Star-Spangled Banner"—on the Opera House stage as Columbia in a suffrage pageant on May 2, 1913 (*left,* with Inez Mulholland as Justice and Pauline Frederick as the Spirit of Woman). But there was another side to the story, as appears from the poster bearing an address two blocks east of the Metropolitan.

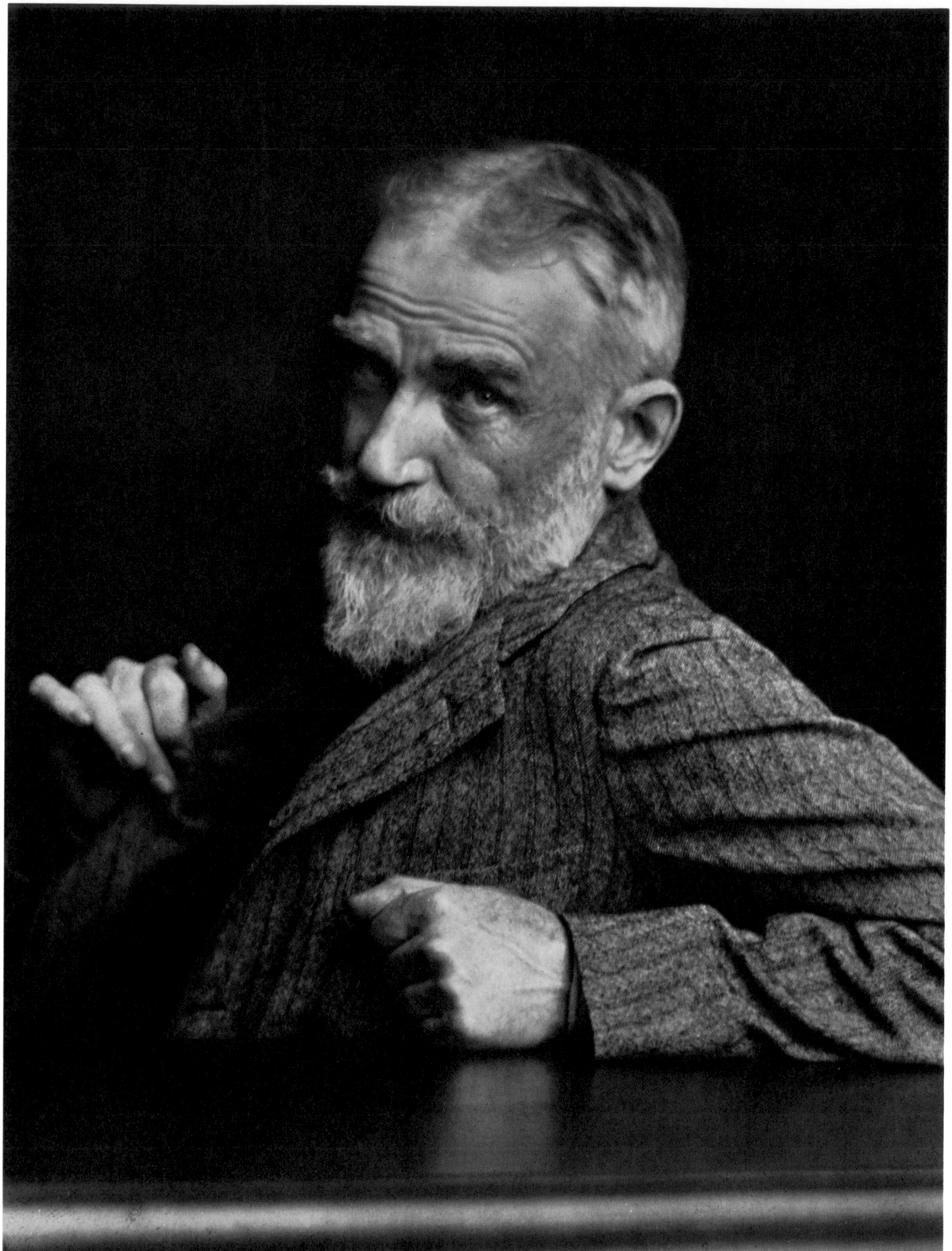

George Bernard Shaw, Mrs. Patrick Campbell: The beautiful actress graced the Opera House boards on May 2, 1905, as part of a farewell testimonial to her colleague Modjeska. Her sometime suitor followed her in 1933 as guest of the Academy of Political Science, whose meeting, held in the Metropolitan, he saluted by confessing that in these surroundings he felt an almost uncontrollable urge to sing.

Ballet Theatre and Ballet Russe: To the Opera
House in 1942 Sol Hurok brought the
memorable dance performances of
Alicia Markova and Hugh Laing in
Delius's *Romeo and Juliet* and Nora
Kaye in *Pillar of Fire*, to Schoenberg music
(*opposite page*). Beginning seven years earlier,
Hurok had booked the Ballets Russes de
Monte Carlo into the Metropolitan, offering not
only standard fare but a number of
non-Russian novelties—Agnes de Mille and
Frederick Franklin in Aaron Copland's *Rodeo*,
for example (*left*), and Franklin and
Alexandra Danilova in Offenbach's *Gaîté
Parisienne* (*below*).

Stars of Moscow and London: Maya Plisetskaya's performance of the Dying Swan (*left*), choreographed by Fokine to the Saint-Saëns music, was a highlight of the Bolshoi Ballet's sensational second season at the Metropolitan Opera House, 1962. One year later Rudolf Nureyev, who had defected from Leningrad's Kirov Ballet during a visit to Paris, was cheered on the same stage for his *Giselle* with Margot Fonteyn, seen opposite in Act II.

Appendices

Index

Picture Credits

General Managers

of the resident opera Company at the Metropolitan Opera House

SEASONS	
1883–84	Henry E. Abbey
1884–85	Leopold Damrosch (died 2/15/85)
1886–91	Edmund C. Stanton
1891–92	Henry E. Abbey Maurice Grau John B. Schoeffel
(1892–93)	(season omitted due to fire)
1893–97	Henry E. Abbey (died 10/17/96) Maurice Grau John B. Schoeffel
(1897–98)	(season omitted due to Abbey's death and reorganization under Grau; guest season by Damrosch-Ellis Company)
1898–1903	Maurice Grau
1903–08	Heinrich Conried
1908–10	Giulio Gatti-Casazza Andreas Dippel
1910–35	Giulio Gatti-Casazza
1935–50	Herbert Witherspoon (died 5/10/35) Edward Johnson
1950—	Rudolf Bing

Operas

performed by the resident Company at the Metropolitan Opera House 1883-1966

TITLE	COMPOSER	FIRST PERFORMANCE
Adriana Lecouvreur	Francesco Cilèa	11/18/07 (opening night)
Die Aegyptische Helena	Richard Strauss	11/6/28 (U.S. premiere)
L'Africaine	Giacomo Meyerbeer	12/7/88 (in German)
Aida	Giuseppe Verdi	11/12/86 (in German)
Alceste	Christoph Willibald von Gluck	1/24/41
Alessandro Stradella	Friedrich von Flotow	2/4/10
Amelia al Ballo (Amelia Goes to the Ball)	Gian Carlo Menotti	3/3/38 (in English)
L'Amico Fritz	Pietro Mascagni	11/15/23
L'Amore dei Tre Re	Italo Montemezzi	1/2/14 (U.S. premiere)
L'Amore Medico	Ermanno Wolf-Ferrari	3/25/14 (U.S. premiere)
Andrea Chénier	Umberto Giordano	3/7/21
Anima Allegra	Franco Vittadini	2/14/23 (U.S. premiere)
Arabella	Richard Strauss	2/10/55 (U.S. premiere)
Ariadne auf Naxos	Richard Strauss	12/19/62 (Prologue in English)
Ariane et Barbe-Bleue	Paul Dukas	3/29/11 (U.S. premiere)
Armide	Christoph Willibald von Gluck	11/14/10 (U.S. premiere) (opening night)
Asrael	Alberto Franchetti	11/26/90 (in German) (U.S. premiere) (opening night)
Un Ballo in Maschera	Giuseppe Verdi	12/11/89 (in German)
Der Barbier von Bagdad	Peter Cornelius	1/3/90 (U.S. premiere)
Il Barbiere di Siviglia	Gioacchino Rossini	11/23/83
Boccaccio	Franz von Suppé	1/2/31
La Bohème	Giacomo Puccini	12/26/00
Boris Godunov	Modest Moussorgsky	3/19/13 (in Italian) (U.S. premiere)
La Campana Sommersa	Ottorino Respighi	11/24/28 (U.S. premiere)
The Canterbury Pilgrims	Reginald De Koven	3/8/17 (world premiere)
Caponsacchi	Richard Hageman	2/4/37 (U.S. premiere)
Carmen	Georges Bizet	1/9/84 (in Italian)
Cavalleria Rusticana	Pietro Mascagni	12/30/91
La Cena delle Beffe (The Jest)	Umberto Giordano	1/2/26 (U.S. premiere)
Le Cid	Jules Massenet	2/12/97
Cleopatra's Night	Henry Hadley	1/20/21 (world premiere)
I Compagnacci	Primo Riccitelli	1/2/24 (U.S. premiere)
Les Contes d'Hoffmann	Jacques Offenbach	1/11/13
Le Coq d'Or	Nikolai Rimsky-Korsakov	3/6/18 (in French) (U.S. premiere)
Così Fan Tutte	Wolfgang Amadeus Mozart	3/24/22 (U.S. premiere)
Crispino e la Comare	Luigi and Federico Ricci	1/18/19
Cyrano (de Bergerac)	Walter Damrosch	2/27/13 (world premiere)
La Dame Blanche (Die Weisse Dame)	François Boieldieu	2/13/04 (in German)
La Damnation de Faust	Hector Berlioz	12/7/06
Diana von Solange	Ernst II, Duke of Saxe-Coburg Gotha	1/9/91 (U.S. premiere)
Dinorah	Giacomo Meyerbeer	1/29/92
Don Carlos (Don Carlo)	Giuseppe Verdi	12/23/20 (in Italian)
Don Giovanni	Wolfgang Amadeus Mozart	11/28/83
Don Pasquale	Gaetano Donizetti	1/8/00
Donna Juanita	Franz von Suppé	1/2/32
Le Donne Curiose	Ermanno Wolf-Ferrari	1/3/12 (U.S. premiere)
Elaine	Herman Bemberg	12/17/94 (U.S. premiere)
Elektra	Richard Strauss	12/3/32
L'Elisir d'Amore	Gaetano Donizetti	1/23/04
The Emperor Jones	Louis Gruenberg	1/7/33 (world premiere)

Note: Works are listed under their original titles; where the Metropolitan or general usage has given an alternate, this is shown in parentheses. The language of the performance is given only if it is not the original.

309

Die Entführung aus dem Serail (The Abduction from the Seraglio)	Wolfgang Amadeus Mozart	11/29/46 (in English)
Ernani	Giuseppe Verdi	1/28/03
Ero e Leandro	Luigi Mancinelli	3/10/99 (U.S. premiere)
Eugene Onegin	Peter Ilich Tchaikovsky	3/24/20 (in Italian) (U.S. stage premiere)
Euryanthe	Carl Maria von Weber	12/23/87 (U.S. premiere)
The Fair at Sorochintsy	Modest Moussorgsky	11/29/30 (in Italian) (U.S. premiere)
Falstaff	Giuseppe Verdi	2/4/95 (U.S. premiere)
La Fanciulla del West	Giacomo Puccini	12/10/10 (world premiere)
Faust	Charles Gounod	10/22/83 (in Italian) (opening of the Metropolitan Opera House)
La Favorite (La Favorita)	Gaetano Donizetti	11/29/95 (in Italian)
Fedora	Umberto Giordano	12/5/06 (U.S. premiere)
Fernand Cortez	Giacomo Meyerbeer	1/6/88 (in German) (U.S. premiere)
Fidelio	Ludwig van Beethoven	11/19/84
La Fille du Régiment	Gaetano Donizetti	1/6/02
Die Fledermaus	Johann Strauss	2/16/05
Der Fliegende Holländer	Richard Wagner	12/31/90
La Forza del Destino	Giuseppe Verdi	11/15/18
Fra Diavolo	Daniel François Auber	2/5/10
Fra Gherardo	Ildebrando Pizzetti	3/21/29 (U.S. premiere)
Francesca da Rimini	Riccardo Zandonai	12/22/16 (U.S. premiere)
Der Freischütz	Carl Maria von Weber	11/24/84
Germania	Alberto Franchetti	1/22/10 (U.S. premiere)
Gianni Schicchi	Giacomo Puccini	12/14/18 (world premiere)
La Gioconda	Amilcare Ponchielli	12/20/83 (U.S. premiere)
I Gioielli della Madonna	Ermanno Wolf-Ferrari	12/12/25
Giovanni Gallurese	Italo Montemezzi	2/19/25 (U.S. premiere)
Das Goldene Kreuz	Ignaz Brüll	11/19/86
Götterdämmerung	Richard Wagner	1/25/88 (U.S. stage premiere)
Goyescas	Enrique Granados	1/28/16 (world premiere) (first opera in Spanish at the Metropolitan)
Guillaume Tell (William Tell)	Gioacchino Rossini	11/28/84 (in German)
La Habanera	Raoul Laparra	1/2/24
Hamlet	Ambroise Thomas	3/10/84 (in Italian)
Hänsel und Gretel	Engelbert Humperdinck	11/25/05
L'Heure Espagnole	Maurice Ravel	11/7/25
Les Huguenots	Giacomo Meyerbeer	3/19/84 (in Italian)
In the Pasha's Garden	John Laurence Seymour	1/24/35 (world premiere)
Iphigénie en Tauride	Christoph Willibald von Gluck	11/25/16 (in German) (U.S. premiere)
Iris	Pietro Mascagni	12/6/07
The Island God	Gian Carlo Menotti	2/20/42 (world premiere)
L'Italiana in Algerì	Gioacchino Rossini	12/5/19
Jenufa	Leoš Janáček	12/6/24 (in German) (U.S. premiere)
Jonny Spielt Auf	Ernst Krenek	1/19/29 (U.S. premiere)
La Juive	Fromental Halévy	1/16/85 (in German)
Julien	Gustave Charpentier	2/26/14 (U.S. premiere)
Khovanshchina	Modest Moussorgsky	2/16/50 (in English)
The King's Henchman	Deems Taylor	2/17/27 (world premiere)

Die Königin von Saba (The Queen of Sheba)	Karl Goldmark	12/2/85 (U.S. premiere)
Königskinder	Engelbert Humperdinck	12/28/10 (world premiere)
Lakmé	Léo Delibes	2/22/92
The Last Savage	Gian Carlo Menotti	1/23/64 (U.S. premiere)
The Legend	Joseph Breil	3/12/19 (world premiere)
Linda di Chamounix	Gaetano Donizetti	3/1/34
Lobetanz	Ludwig Thuille	11/18/11 (U.S. premiere)
Lodoletta	Pietro Mascagni	1/12/18 (U.S. premiere)
Lohengrin	Richard Wagner	11/7/83 (in Italian)
Loreley	Alfredo Catalani	3/4/22
Louise	Gustave Charpentier	1/15/21
Lucia di Lammermoor	Gaetano Donizetti	10/24/83
Lucrezia Borgia	Gaetano Donizetti	12/5/04
Luisa Miller	Giuseppe Verdi	12/21/29
Die Lustigen Weiber von Windsor (The Merry Wives of Windsor)	Otto Nicolai	3/9/00
Macbeth	Giuseppe Verdi	2/5/59
Madama Butterfly	Giacomo Puccini	2/11/07
Madame Sans-Gêne	Umberto Giordano	1/25/15 (world premiere)
Madeleine	Victor Herbert	1/24/14 (world premiere)
Madonna Imperia	Franco Alfano	2/8/28 (U.S. premiere)
The Man Without a Country	Walter Damrosch	5/12/37 (world premiere)
Manon	Jules Massenet	1/16/95
Manon Lescaut	Giacomo Puccini	1/18/07
Manru	Ignace Jan Paderewski	2/14/02 (U.S. premiere)
Marouf	Henri Rabaud	12/19/17 (U.S. premiere)
Martha	Friedrich von Flotow	3/14/84 (in Italian)
Il Matrimonio Segreto (The Clandestine Marriage)	Domenico Cimarosa	2/25/37 (in English)
Mefistofele	Arrigo Boito	12/5/83
Die Meistersinger von Nürnberg	Richard Wagner	1/4/86 (U.S. premiere)
Merlin	Karl Goldmark	1/3/87 (U.S. premiere)
Merry Mount	Howard Hanson	2/10/34 (world stage premiere)
[*Messa da Requiem*	Giuseppe Verdi	2/17/01]
Messaline	Isidore de Lara	1/22/02 (U.S. premiere)
Mignon	Ambroise Thomas	10/31/83 (in Italian)
Mireille	Charles Gounod	2/28/19
Mona	Horatio Parker	3/14/12 (world premiere)
Mona Lisa	Max von Schillings	3/1/23 (U.S. premiere)
La Muette de Portici (Masaniello)	Daniel François Auber	12/29/84 (in German)
Nabucco	Giuseppe Verdi	10/24/60
La Navarraise	Jules Massenet	12/11/95 (U.S. premiere)
Norma	Vincenzo Bellini	2/27/90 (in German)
La Notte di Zoraima	Italo Montemezzi	12/2/31 (U.S. premiere)
Le Nozze di Figaro	Wolfgang Amadeus Mozart	1/31/94
Oberon	Carl Maria von Weber	12/28/18
L'Oiseau Bleu (The Blue Bird)	Albert Wolff	12/27/19 (world premiere)
L'Oracolo	Franco Leoni	2/4/15 (U.S. premiere)
Orfeo ed Euridice	Christoph Willibald von Gluck	12/30/91
Otello	Giuseppe Verdi	1/11/92
Pagliacci	Ruggiero Leoncavallo	12/11/93
Parsifal	Richard Wagner	12/24/03 (U.S. stage premiere)
Les Pêcheurs de Perles	Georges Bizet	1/11/96 (incomplete)
Pelléas et Mélisande	Claude Debussy	3/21/25
La Périchole	Jacques Offenbach	12/21/56 (in English)
Peter Grimes	Benjamin Britten	2/12/48
Peter Ibbetson	Deems Taylor	2/7/31 (world premiere)
Philémon et Baucis	Charles Gounod	11/29/93
Phoebus and Pan	Johann Sebastian Bach	1/15/42 (in English)
The Pipe of Desire	Frederick S. Converse	3/18/10 (first American opera at the Metropolitan and first opera in English)
Pique Dame	Peter Ilich Tchaikovsky	3/5/10 (in German) (first Russian opera staged in N.Y.)
Der Polnische Jude (The Polish Jew)	Karel Weiss	3/9/21 (in English) (U.S. premiere)
Le Preziose Ridicole	Felice Lattuada	12/10/30 (U.S. premiere)
Prodaná Nevesta (The Bartered Bride)	Bedrich Smetana	2/19/09 (in German)
Prince Igor	Alexander Borodin	12/30/15 (in Italian) (U.S. premiere)
Le Prophète	Giacomo Meyerbeer	3/21/84 (in Italian)
I Puritani	Vincenzo Bellini	10/29/83

The Rake's Progress	Igor Stravinsky	2/14/53 (U.S. premiere)
La Reine Fiammette	Xavier Leroux	1/24/19 (U.S. premiere)
Das Rheingold	Richard Wagner	1/4/89 (U.S. premiere)
Rienzi	Richard Wagner	2/5/86
Rigoletto	Giuseppe Verdi	1/2/85 (in German)
Robert le Diable	Giacomo Meyerbeer	11/19/83 (in Italian)
Le Roi de Lahore	Jules Massenet	2/29/24
Le Roi d'Ys	Edouard Lalo	1/5/22
Roméo et Juliette	Charles Gounod	12/14/91 (opening night)
La Rondine	Giacomo Puccini	3/10/28 (U.S. premiere)
Der Rosenkavalier	Richard Strauss	12/9/13 (U.S. premiere)
Le Rossignol	Igor Stravinsky	3/6/26 (in French) (U.S. premiere)
Sadko	Nikolai Rimsky-Korsakov	1/25/30 (in French) (U.S. premiere)
St. Elizabeth	Franz Liszt	1/3/18 (in English) (U.S. stage premiere)
Salammbô	Ernest Reyer	3/20/01
Salome	Richard Strauss	1/22/07 (U.S. premiere)
Samson et Dalila	Camille Saint-Saëns	2/8/95
Il Segreto di Susanna	Ermanno Wolf-Ferrari	12/13/12
Semiramide	Gioacchino Rossini	1/12/94
La Serva Padrona	Giovanni Battista Pergolesi	2/23/35
Shanewis	Charles Wakefield Cadman	3/23/18 (world premiere)
Siegfried	Richard Wagner	11/9/87 (U.S. premiere)
Il Signor Bruschino	Gioacchino Rossini	12/9/32 (U.S. premiere)
Simon Boccanegra	Giuseppe Verdi	1/28/32 (U.S. premiere)
Snegurochka (The Snow Maiden)	Nikolai Rimsky-Korsakov	1/23/22 (in French) (U.S. premiere)
La Sonnambula	Vincenzo Bellini	11/14/83
Suor Angelica	Giacomo Puccini	12/14/18 (world premiere)
Svanda Dudák *(Schwanda der Dudelsackpfeifer)*	Jaromir Weinberger	11/7/31 (in German) (U.S. premiere)
Il Tabarro	Giacomo Puccini	12/14/18 (world premiere)
Tannhäuser	Richard Wagner	11/17/84 (opening night)
The Temple Dancer	John Adam Hugo	3/12/19 (world premiere)
Thaïs	Jules Massenet	2/16/17
Tiefland	Eugen d'Albert	11/23/08 (U.S. premiere)
Tosca	Giacomo Puccini	2/4/01 (U.S. premiere)
Die Tote Stadt	Erich Wolfgang Korngold	11/19/21 (U.S. premiere)
La Traviata	Giuseppe Verdi	11/5/83
Tristan und Isolde	Richard Wagner	12/1/86 (U.S. premiere)
Der Trompeter von Säckingen	Viktor Ernst Nessler	11/23/87 (U.S. premiere)
Il Trovatore	Giuseppe Verdi	10/26/83
Turandot	Giacomo Puccini	11/16/26 (U.S. premiere)
Vanessa	Samuel Barber	1/15/58 (world premiere)
Il Vassallo di Szigeth	Antonio Smareglia	12/12/90 (in German) (U.S. premiere)
Versiegelt	Leo Blech	1/20/12 (U.S. premiere)
La Vestale	Gasparo Spontini	11/12/25 (in Italian)
La Vida Breve	Manuel de Falla	3/6/26 (U.S. premiere)
Le Villi	Giacomo Puccini	12/17/08 (U.S. premiere)
Violanta	Erich Wolfgang Korngold	11/5/27 (U.S. premiere)
Der Wald	Ethel Smyth	3/11/03 (U.S. premiere)
Die Walküre	Richard Wagner	1/30/85
La Wally	Alfredo Catalani	1/6/09 (U.S. premiere)
The Warrior	Bernard Rogers	1/11/47 (world premiere)
Werther	Jules Massenet	4/19/94
Der Widerspenstigen Zähmung *(The Taming of the Shrew)*	Hermann Goetz	3/15/16
Wozzeck	Alban Berg	3/5/59 (in English)
Die Zauberflöte (The Magic Flute)	Wolfgang Amadeus Mozart	3/30/00 (in Italian)
Zazà	Ruggiero Leoncavallo	1/16/20
Der Zigeunerbaron (The Gypsy Baron)	Johann Strauss	2/15/06

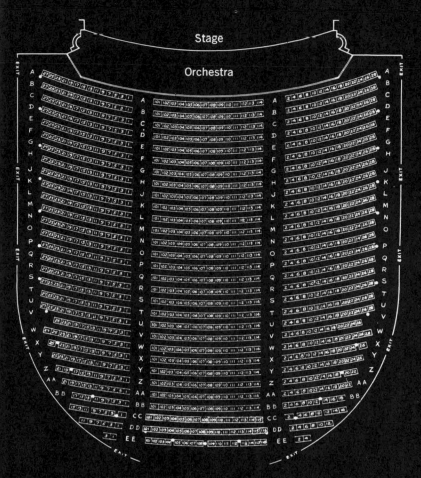

Stage

Orchestra

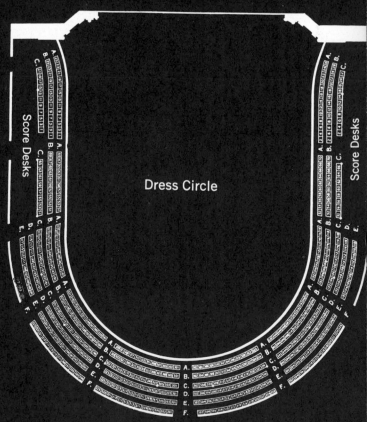

Parterre Boxes
Eight seats

Score Desks

Dress Circle

Score Desks

Seating Diagrams of the
Metropolitan Opera House

Here are the six levels of the Metropolitan Opera
House as it stood at the end of its career. Since these
diagrams were designed for selling tickets rather
than as architectural blueprints, they are not uniform
in scale throughout.

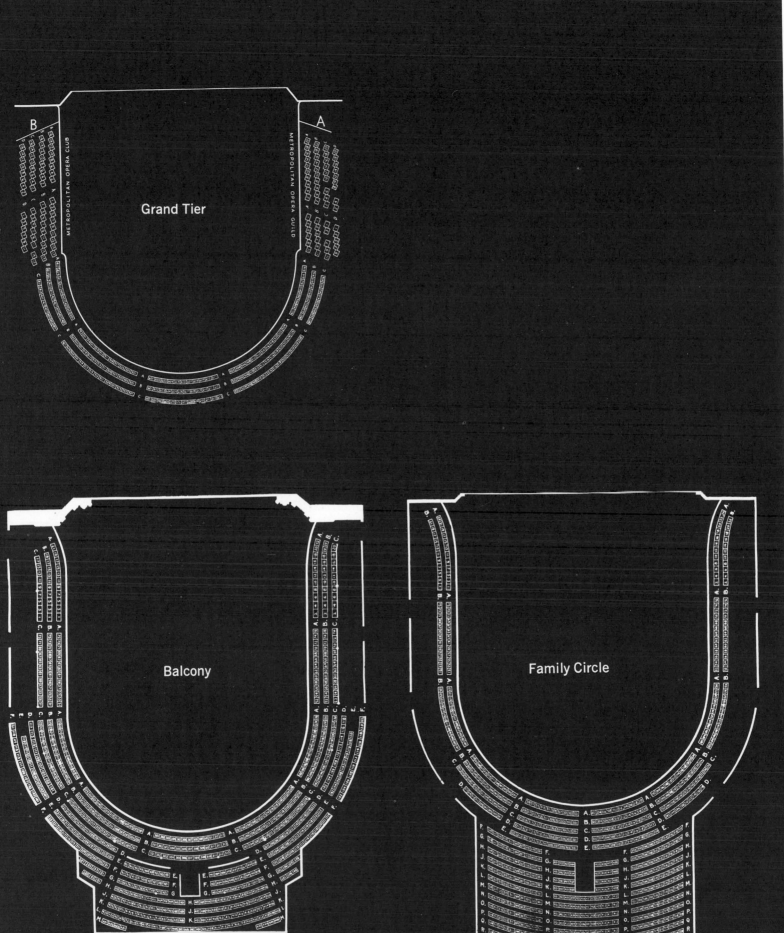

Grand Tier

Balcony

Family Circle

(Figures in italics indicate an illustration.)

Picture Credits

The authors are indebted to Mrs. August Belmont for the portrait by Bachrach on page 189, to Mrs. Arthur M. Reis for the production photographs of *Le Sacre du Printemps* on page 284, *Oedipus Rex* on page 286, and *Les Noces* on page 287. Thanks are also due to Reginald Allen for the diagram on page 190, to George Balanchine for the painting on page 196, to Walter Toscanini for the drawing on page 98 and the right-hand photograph on page 123.

The sources for the remaining pictures are as follows:

American Museum of Natural History: 15 top

Associated Press: 273 bottom

Bettmann Archive: 17 bottom, 28 left, 33 bottom, 115 bottom, 116, 121, 149 top, 174 top

Brown Brothers: 17 top, 28 top, 59, 61, 82, 83 top and bottom, 86, 90, 95 top, 98 top, 100 top, 117 top, 119, 157 bottom, 179 bottom, 191, 201, 289 top right, 294 top and top left, 295 right, 296

Lowell Chereskin: 259

Columbia University, Urban Collection: 134, 146, 147

Eugene Cook: 216, 218, 219, 220 top, 224, 225, 226, 228, 230, 231, 242, 243, 248, 249, 260, 262-63, 264 right, 272

Country Life: 19

Thomas Y. Crowell Co.: 165

Culver Pictures: 28 right, 30, 35 right, 57 top, 58, 80 top and right, 81, 87, 91 top, 92, 99, 100 bottom, 101, 105, 114, 115 top, 123, 125, 126, 135, 139, 141, 143, 149 bottom, 150, 151 left, 155, 157 top, 163, 173, 178 bottom, 179 top, 181, 183 top, 186, 187, 213 bottom, 285 (by Soichi Sunami), 293, 294 top right, 295 left

Discoteca: 151 right

Frank Dunand: 237, 240, 253, 254-55

Elliott Erwitt: 223

Fred Fehl: 300, 301

Alexandre Georges: 69, 70, 71, 72, 73, 74, 75, 76 top, 77, 207, 220 bottom, 221, 256, 279 bottom

Irwin Goldstein: 278

Harper & Row: 196 bottom, 197

Harvard Theatre Collection: 22, 25 bottom, 29, 33 top, 34, 38-39, 42, 44 bottom left, 45 top and right, 49 top, 64 top, 67, 178 top, 289 left and bottom, 290 left, 291, 292, 294 bottom, 295 bottom, 299

Tom Hollyman: 274-75

Sedge LeBlang: 183 bottom, 264 left

Frank Lerner: 251 top

Life: 241, 258 bottom, 273 top

Harvey Lloyd: 244-45

Macmillan Co.: 49 bottom

Metropolitan Opera Archives: 24, 27, 43 left, 54 top, 83 middle, 103, 104, 106-107, 108-109, 110, 111, 113, 128, 129, 130, 132, 133, 142 top, 158, 170-71, 177, 182, 185, 192-93, 211, 290 top and right

Duane Michals: 257

Museum of the City of New York, Byron Collection: 60, 62, 63, 64 bottom, 85, 131, 288

Museum of Modern Art: 131

Musical America: 48 top, 89, 96, 117 bottom, 136, 142 left, 145, 148, 152-53, 162, 286 top

New-York Historical Society: 31

New York *News*: 238-39

Opera News: 14, 15, 16, 20, 21, 25 top, 32, 35 top and left, 36, 41, 43 right, 44 top and right, 45 left, 46-47, 48 bottom, 50, 52-53, 54 left and bottom, 55, 57 bottom, 65, 66, 78, 80 bottom, 88, 91 bottom, 93, 94, 95 bottom, 122, 127, 138, 142 bottom, 154, 156, 160-61, 164, 167, 168, 169, 174 bottom, 175, 194, 199, 200 top, 203, 204, 205, 206, 208-209, 210, 212, 215, 297

Tony Ray-Jones: 76 bottom, 227, 233, 279 top

Arnold Rosenberg: 200 bottom, 250

Paul Seligman: 232, 235, 236, 247, 251 bottom, 270, 271, 277

Wayne J. Shilkret: 302, 303

Vernon L. Smith: 246, 252, 258 top, 261, 265, 266, 267

Charles Gary Solin: 276

Edward Steichen: 176, 283

Martha Swope: 229, 268-69

Vogue: 298

"Weegee": 213 top, 214, 215